Strategic Studies Institute
and
U.S. Army War College Press

WAR AND INSURGENCY IN THE WESTERN SAHARA

Geoffrey Jensen

May 2013

*****

*****

Comments pertaining to this report are invited and should be forwarded to: Director, Strategic Studies Institute and U.S. Army War College Press, U.S. Army War College, 47 Ashburn Drive, Carlisle, PA 17013-5010.

*****

Many thanks to Colonel Pedro Baños Bajo, Dr. Guillem Colom Piella, Colonel Ignacio Fuente Cobo, Dr. Bradley Coleman, Dr. Shannon Fleming, Dr. Benjamin Fordham, Dr. Clifford Kiracofe, Dr. Martin Loicano, and Jesús M. Pérez, who assisted me in varied ways as I researched and wrote this monograph. Of course, I alone am responsible for the opinions expressed and any errors contained within.

I dedicate this work to the late Jorge Aspizua Turrión, whom I greatly miss as a friend, confidant, and source of ideas.

*****

FOREWORD

As a major non-North Atlantic Treaty Organization ally, Morocco enjoys a close relationship with the United States that has only strengthened in recent years. Not only is Morocco considered a stable, liberalizing, and democratizing Arab Muslim country, but it has also been an important partner in combating terrorism and pursuing peace in the Middle East. It receives more U.S. foreign assistance than any other country in the Maghreb, and the U.S. Army will continue to participate in many activities, including major exercises and smaller security-oriented activities, meant to build partner capacity and maintain good relations.

Yet, even after decades marked by war, significant military and diplomatic involvement by the United States, and long-term intervention by the United Nations, no resolution is in sight to Morocco's conflict with Western Saharan nationalists. This monograph, completed by Dr. Jensen in September 2012, demonstrates the history of the dispute—characterized by insurgency, regular warfare, intifadas, and the longest functional military barrier in the world—and offers lessons of relevance to military planners and policymakers alike.

DOUGLAS C. LOVELACE, JR.
Director
Strategic Studies Institute and
    U.S. Army War College Press

ABOUT THE AUTHOR

GEOFFREY JENSEN has taught at Yale, UCLA, the University of Southern Mississippi, and the Royal Military Academy Sandhurst. He now holds the John C. Biggs '30 Cincinnati Chair in Military History at the Virginia Military Institute in Lexington, Virginia. He is the author of various works on modern Europe, colonial North Africa, and military history. Dr. Jensen holds a B.A. from Indiana University and an M.A. and Ph.D. from Yale University.

SUMMARY

At a crucial crossroads between Africa and Europe, the Mediterranean and the Atlantic, and the "Arab World" and the West, Morocco has long had a special place in U.S. diplomacy and strategic planning. Since the terrorist attacks of September 11, 2001, Morocco's importance to the United States has only risen, and the more recent uncertainties of the Arab Spring and Islamist extremism in Africa have further increased the strategic value and operational relevance of the Moroccan-American alliance. Yet, one of the pillars of the legitimacy of the Moroccan monarchy, its claim to Western Sahara, remains a point of violent contention. Since the Spanish withdrawal and subsequent occupation of the territory by Morocco in 1975, the United States has poured many millions of dollars in materiel, training, and intelligence into the Moroccan armed forces. But the latter has failed to inflict a decisive defeat on the Polisario Front, the Western Saharan organization whose goal is full independence for Western Sahara.

This monograph provides an historical analysis of the conflict in Western Sahara, stressing developments of relevance to the U.S. Army and to American and regional strategic interests since Morocco's independence in 1956. Points of emphasis include evolving human and physical geography; the role of the United States, Algeria, and other outside powers in the conflict; and military tactics, operations, and strategies. The monograph also analyzes the current situation in the region and makes recommendations for U.S. policy and military planning.

Host to valuable natural resources and the largest functioning military barrier in the world, the Western

Sahara has seen intifada-style resistance to Moroccan occupation since the mid-1990s. Communications and coordination between the pro-independence Polisario sympathizers in the "liberated" and "occupied" territories and in refugee camps in Algeria—facilitated in no small part by the Internet—have also increased, especially among the increasingly radicalized Sahrawi youth, who appear to have lost faith in the Polisario leadership even as they continue to embrace its basic anti-Moroccan outlook. In the meantime, terrorist and criminal elements threaten to infiltrate the territory and the camps in Algeria.

One cannot understand the Polisario insurgency's socio-cultural roots, military achievements, or the reason why both sides eventually settled on a ceasefire without a good grasp of Western Saharan physical and human geography, neither of which has remained static. In fact, changes in both created the conditions for the insurgency and enabled it to develop so successfully. At the same time, Morocco's slowly-learned ability to respond to and alter geographical conditions helped bring about the ceasefire of 1991, even though Morocco's actions also made a long-term solution more elusive in some ways.

Natural resources have shaped human geography, outside interests, and insurgent movements in Western Sahara since the Spanish period, and they may influence long-term U.S. interests in the region. Morocco's expansion into Western Sahara did not stem from the mineral resources there, but Morocco stands to gain from their full exploitation. The desire to develop the economic potential offered by Western Saharan geography began to grow in earnest after the discovery of large phosphate deposits by the Spaniards after World War II. Fishing and the potential for oil exploitation have also shaped the development of the region and the evolving strategic interests of the major players.

Although complicated questions of ethnicity, history, and cultural traditions make generalizations about Sahrawis difficult, a complete picture of the conflict entails a good understanding of the origins and development of Western Saharan identity, from which has emerged one of the world's youngest but most vigorous nationalist movements. The lack of agreement on the fundamental question of what constitutes a Sahrawi complicates the efforts of the United Nations (UN) and others to find reliable census figures or organize a plebiscite.

The popular appeal of the concept of "Greater Morocco" goes far to explain why Rabat has resisted outside pressures and refuses to compromise on the issue, even after the military and financial costs of occupying the territory contributed to considerable social unrest. In October 1957, the newly independent Moroccan state officially adopted the ideology of Greater Morocco, and the `Alawi dynasty has staked its legitimacy in part on the preservation of its "southern provinces," as it calls Western Sahara. As a component of Moroccan national identity, the belief that Western Sahara is an integral part of Morocco enjoyed widespread domestic support, although the human and financial costs of the war against the Polisario also has had some negative impact on the regime's popularity.

Historically, Spanish control over the territory rested on a relatively effective system of military occupation and administration, but Spanish military authorities failed to grasp how changing geographical and social conditions fomented the rise of nationalist resistance, especially among younger Sahrawis. Spanish military responses to the rise of Sahrawi nationalism and unrest among the youth exacerbated the growing conflict.

After the Spanish withdrawal from the territory in 1975, Morocco waged a brutal military campaign against the Polisario, and large numbers of people fled to refugee camps, where traditional tribal identities softened and Sahrawi national consciousness grew. In the meantime, the Polisario's early military successes against Morocco and its ally, Mauritania, defied expectations. The reasons for the Polisario's survival included its access to outside support and sanctuaries (mainly Algeria), Moroccan mistakes, and Mauritanian weaknesses. Also crucial were the strategic thought of Polisario's military leadership and the tactical skills of its soldiers, their high level of morale, and their ability to use geography to their advantage. The Mauritanian armed forces disposed of relatively few human and materiel resources, withdrawing from the war in 1979 after suffering repeated attacks by the Polisario, including some deep inside Mauritania. Although they continued to fight, the Moroccan armed forces revealed ineffectiveness and operational shortcomings against the guerrilla tactics of the Polisario on various occasions.

After the repeated tactical failings of the Moroccan armed forces began to gain strategic significance, the United States greatly increased its contribution to the fight against the Polisario. After the fall of the Shah of Iran and the Polisario's damaging attacks within Morocco, Washington wanted to make sure that it did not lose another strategic ally in Africa and the Middle East. Beginning in 1981, Morocco began construction of the largest functional military barrier in the world, "the Berm," a very expensive enterprise that eventually allowed the country to occupy and control about

80 percent of the Western Sahara. The decision to erect the Berm signaled an acknowledgement by Moroccan leaders that decisive defeat of the Polisario was not possible; hence, Rabat adopted a strategy of static defense. Ten years later, the Berm facilitated the UN-brokered ceasefire, which occurred after both sides, thoroughly exhausted, realized that they could not achieve decisive victory. Thereafter, the struggle continued in the diplomatic sphere.

In the occupied territory, Morocco spent much money on security and economic development, but devoted virtually no efforts to winning the hearts and minds of the Sahrawi people. It also imported large numbers of people from Morocco, in part with the hope of thereby foiling the Polisario's prediction that it would win a referendum on the future status of the territory. UN envoy James Baker exerted considerable efforts trying to reach a settlement, but in the wake of Moroccan intransigence and Washington's unwillingness to pressure Rabat, he resigned in 2003.

In the meantime, dissatisfaction has grown in the refugee camps and the occupied territory, especially among the younger Sahrawis. Many express impatience and disappointment with the traditional Polisario elites and their failure to make gains on the diplomatic front. This dissatisfaction has manifested itself in intifada-style protests. Recent kidnappings and arrests suggest that terrorist and criminal organizations, some with ties to al-Qaeda, are attempting to infiltrate Western Sahara and the refugee camps, although Polisario leaders appear to be trying to keep them out. Still, such infiltrations may come to threaten regional security.

Given the importance of Moroccan stability and the threat that increased terrorist activity in the region would pose to the United States and Europe, Washington has a strong interest in promoting a solution to the Western Sahara problem. In theory, a solution could be reached that has something to offer all of the immediately affected parties (Morocco, the Polisario Front, and Algeria). But Europe will need to play a leading role in propelling negotiations; the United States should consider ways to leverage European countries to do so. In the meantime, the United States should continue to monitor closely the security situation in Western Sahara, which has relevance to current U.S. Africa Command (AFRICOM) activities. At the same time, the United States should take advantage of the relatively Western-friendly, modern outlooks among many Polisario leaders and other Sahrawis, who are less susceptible to radical Islamist appeals.

The U.S. Army should use the military history of Western Sahara as a source of concrete lessons, in particular with regard to guerrilla tactics and the role of fortified walls (the Berm) in counterinsurgency and static defense in general. The U.S. Army should also learn more about the Moroccan military and prepare for the possibility of more joint operations. In addition to learning about the Polisario's tactical, operational, and strategic successes and failures, U.S. military planners should also take into account the strengths and limitations of the Moroccan armed forces and adjust their expectations accordingly.

As the history of the region illustrates, the Western Sahara problem defies easy solutions. On the other hand, the situation there is not without hope. With proper, historically informed policy decisions and appropriate leveraging by the United States, a solution-that has something to offer all the interested parties may well be possible.

WAR AND INSURGENCY IN THE WESTERN SAHARA

INTRODUCTION

At a crucial crossroads between Africa and Europe, the Mediterranean and the Atlantic, and the "Arab World" and the West, Morocco has long had a special place in U.S. diplomacy and strategic planning. Since the terrorist attacks of September 11, 2001 (9/11), Morocco's importance to the United States has only increased; in 2004, President George W. Bush designated the country as a "major non-NATO [North Atlantic Treaty Organization] ally," thereby conferring it with various financial and military benefits not otherwise available to non-NATO states. More recently, the Moroccan regime has faced new risks to its stability, including Arab Spring-related developments and, to the south, possible threats from the Sahel region — which joins North and West Africa and spans historic trade and migration routes. These threats have taken the form of Islamist terrorism, the drug trade, kidnapping, and other criminal activities.

In the meantime, one of the pillars of the legitimacy of Morocco's Alawi dynasty, its claim to Western Sahara, remains a point of violent contention. Occupied by Morocco after Spain's withdrawal in 1975, the territory saw open war between Western Saharan nationalists, supported by Algeria, Libya, and other foreign powers, and the Moroccan armed forces until the 1991 ceasefire. Since then, Western Sahara has remained divided between "occupied" and "liberated" zones, which are separated by the largest functional military barrier in the world — sort of a Moroccan version of the Bar Lev Line, consisting of sand walls and a sophisticated net of sensors, mines, barbed wire, and weaponry.

1

The many millions of dollars in materiel, training, intelligence, and advisors that the United States contributed to Morocco's war in the Western Sahara, along with the actions of major American diplomatic players in the conflict—from Vernon Walters to James Baker to Hillary Clinton—underscore the strategic importance of the region. Indeed, the United States gave more economic and military aid to Morocco than to any other African country since the end of World War II, with the exception of Egypt. Tellingly, between 1950 and 1983, over 90 percent of U.S. arms deliveries to Morocco occurred during the first 7 years of the Western Sahara war.[1] More recently, the territory, known to Moroccans as the "southern provinces," has hosted intifada-style protests, violent confrontations, continued repression by Moroccan authorities, and growing discontent among the younger generation. The immense Sahrawi refugee camps just across the Algerian border have seen kidnappings and infiltration attempts by al-Qaeda associated organizations.

The Western Sahara conflict merits attention for other reasons as well. The territory has valuable natural resources, including phosphates, fishing, and possibly large amounts of oil. The territory also remains a major point of contention between Morocco and Algeria, whose cooperation is necessary to combat regional security threats but who remain separated by one of the longest closed borders in the world. In the sphere of international relations, the Western Sahara problem involves fundamental issues of self-determination and sovereignty. According to former U.S. Senator George McGovern, "What ultimately is at stake is the post-World War II international legal system."[2]

This monograph aims to provide an historical overview of the Western Sahara and its strategic importance, with an emphasis on military matters. As will become clear, effective strategic and military decisionmaking about the region entails knowledge of relevant political, geographical, cultural, economic, and social developments and conditions, as well as an understanding of the tactical and operational limitations imposed by these conditions. Although this monograph concludes with a set of specific policy and military planning recommendations, its main goal is to provide an exposition of the Western Sahara problem that will help military and political planners formulate and carry out policy and operations—whatever the strategic goals may be—based on essential historical knowledge and reasonable expectations. The history of Western Sahara can also provide the U.S. Army with learning opportunities about desert counterinsurgency, strategies of static defense, and related tactical and operational methods.

Before beginning that discussion, however, it is worth emphasizing the degree to which political agendas color much of the existing writing about Morocco and Western Sahara. Although such influences are hardly secret, unexpected, or unique to this issue, it nonetheless bears remembering that analyses of the current situation, whether by government officials, academics, or policy think tanks, often serve broader attempts to support or undermine the position of the Moroccan government on the issue. A 2005 report by the Belgian-based European Strategic Intelligence and Security Center, for example, portrayed the Polisario in highly negative terms. But the report relied heavily on the testimony of defectors from the Polisario and ignored more nuanced analyses by outside observers. Even a Moroccan periodical subsequently described the report as "remotely controlled" from Rabat.[3] In a similar example of such contradictions, a U.S. Embassy report and an article based on multiple visits to Western Sahara and "dozens of interviews" describe separatist sentiment as insignificant; the article's authors maintain that "the Polisario's credibility is low" and that "the goal of most Sahrawis is widespread autonomy" rather than full independence.[4] But recent books by experts in the field leave readers with the opposite impression, with one book maintaining that the recent intifada "has allowed many Western Saharans to express their true beliefs, which is support for the cause of independence," and the other describing universal support for independence among Sahrawi refugees.[5] Clearly, there is no consensus.

The intention here is not to accuse any of the authors cited above of misleading their readers in order to promote political agendas. But policymakers should remember that the information found in these and other books, articles, and reports, when used selectively, can make a complicated situation seem more clear-cut than it really is. Sweeping statements about public opinion and major actors, for instance—whether Algeria, U.S. oil companies, or terrorist groups—merit particular scrutiny. Today, the Internet is replete with Web pages about the Western Sahara intended for foreign consumption, often in English, Spanish, and French, and clearly slanted to particular interests. An effective approach to the Western Sahara problem will entail, above all, an understanding of its nuances; accounts that portray the conflict or its players in black and white terms need careful scrutiny.

Historical Overview.

The Western Sahara as a distinct territory with its own identity grew out of a long history of Spanish involvement in the area. For centuries, Spain had shown an interest in northwestern Africa, although along the Atlantic coast, Spaniards made little progress beyond occasional explorations and other limited activities. Nevertheless, at the Berlin Conference of 1884-85, Spain asserted its right to a large swath of territory extending inland from the coast. It based its claim on the small Spanish commercial enterprise at Dakhla, then called Villa Cisneros, which was an outgrowth of facilities established several years earlier to support fishing operations from the Canary Islands.

The territory of Western Sahara (formerly the Spanish Sahara), the entirety of which Spain did not effectively control until the 1930s, consists of some 266,000 square kilometers (km) between a long section of the Atlantic coast and modern-day Mauritania, Algeria, and Morocco, although the latter, of course, does not recognize any border with Western Sahara. The Spanish archipelago of the Canary Islands lies just 100 km off the northern Moroccan-Western Saharan frontier. Unlike much of Greater Sahara, Western Sahara is not entirely covered by sand. In the north, the Saqiyah al-Hamra has deep gullies, and the Guelta Zemmur has large rises and many caves.

Over the years, the geographical characteristics of the northern part of Western Sahara have facilitated guerrilla attacks against security forces, providing cover for insurgent movements and small, scattered base areas. Also in the north, the Ouarkziz Mountains have provided similar opportunities for hiding. The coast of the Western Sahara is rough and cliff-lined; there are ports at Dakhla, La Guera, and to the west of El Aaiún (Laayoune). There is relatively little tradition of fishing among the major Sahrawi groups. Historically, fishermen in the waters off the Saharan coast have often come from the Canary Islands. Although not as conducive to guerrilla activities, the flat, sparsely populated regions to the south are so vast that they have proved difficult for government forces — whether French, Spanish, Mauritanian, or Moroccan — to control fully, even with the benefits of airpower.

In 1912, France and Spain agreed upon the borders for their northwestern African possessions. The French took Algeria and Mauritania and control of the largest portion of the new protectorate of Morocco. The Spanish zones of the Moroccan protectorate were a relatively small slice of territory along the northern coast and what was called "Southern Spanish Morocco," consisting of the Villa Bens area and known as the so-called Tarfaya (or Cape Juby) Strip. Legally speaking, the Moroccan protectorate was not a colony, because the sultan ostensibly remained in power, with France and Spain supposedly administering Morocco on the sultan's behalf. The Spanish Sahara, on the other hand, was a full-fledged colony of Spain. Under French pressure, Spain occupied the Ifni area to the north of Tarfaya in 1934, while the French endeavored to connect key areas in southeastern Morocco, western Algeria (Tindouf), and Mauritania (Zouerate). In this way, the French could encircle the guerrilla movements that had been causing them trouble.[6]

After World War II, Spain established the independent entity of Spanish West Africa, which consisted of three parts: Ifni, Saqiya al Hamra, and Río de Oro; the latter two were often referred to simply as the Spanish

Sahara, or Río de Oro. When Morocco attained independence in 1956, Madrid first hesitated to relinquish any of Spanish West Africa. The Moroccan-supported Liberation Army (LA), later called the Sahrawi Liberation Army by the Spaniards, began to attack French outposts in Algeria and Mauritania, using Spanish territory as a safe haven. The Spanish military, lacking sufficient forces and clear instructions from Madrid, at first let guerrilla bands move across Spanish territory with surprising freedom, although the Spaniards provided the French with information about their movements.[7]

The LA forces, however, found the French to be more than they could handle, and they shifted their efforts to the Spanish-controlled north, sparking the outbreak of the Ifni War (1957-58). The Spaniards fought back hard but eventually withdrew to a defensive parameter around the town of Sidi Ifni. The Spanish adoption of a defensive military strategy stemmed in part from the fear of Spanish dictator Francisco Franco — remembering his experiences in North Africa decades earlier — that Spanish outposts in the interior were too vulnerable.[8] In the Spanish Sahara, Operation HURRICANE, making ample use of paratroopers and involving Spanish and French ground, air, and naval forces, subsequently cleared the bands. The Spaniards then began the task of reestablishing Spanish authority and disarming the nomads who had joined forces with the LA.[9]

In the 1958 Treaty of Angra Cintra, Madrid relinquished the Tarfaya Strip, where Sahrawi nationalism would get its start. In fact, many Spanish observers portray the handing over of this area, which had a relatively sedentary and urban character, as a betrayal by Spain of the indigenous residents, and they trace the origins of Sahrawi nationalism to this act.[10] With the transfer of the territory, Sahrawis discovered that Morocco could be more repressive than the Spaniards had been. A founding leader of the early Sahrawi nationalist movement, Mohamed Sidi Ibrahim Bassiri, moved from the Tarfaya Strip to Smara in Spanish Sahara because he had more freedom of movement there than under repressive Moroccan security forces.[11]

Besides further alienating people in the region, the handing over of the Tarfaya Strip to Morocco seemed to go against possible Spanish economic interests. The territory had offered potential commercial benefits to Spain in the form of fishing and oil resources, and it is strategically situated directly across from the Canary Islands. Furthermore, the area had more in common ethnically and culturally with Spanish Sahara (and less in common with much of Morocco) than did Ifni. Explanations for Spain's acquiescence to Moroccan demands for Tarfaya may include a possible secret agreement over the release of Spanish prisoners from the Ifni War; pressure from the United States, which wanted to bolster the Moroccan monachy; and Moroccan cooperation in cleaning up the LA forces still in the Sahara. The Moroccan king distrusted the LA, many of whose soldiers had refused to join the Moroccan Royal Armed Forces (*Forces Armées Royales,* or FAR) founded in May 1956.[12]

Yet, Madrid had its own reasons for desiring good relations with Morocco, regardless of outside pressures and any possible economic benefits to holding on to the Tarfaya Strip. The Spanish military withdrawal from Morocco was not going to happen overnight, and the general staff and national government in Madrid had an interest in cultivating good relations with Spain's newly independent neighbor across the

Gibraltar Strait. Overall, the relationship between the Spanish army and the embryonic FAR evolved relatively smoothly during this period, and Spanish military personnel stayed for several years during the transition. At the time, the Moroccan independence party, Istiql, even attempted to assuage Spanish concerns over LA forces in the Western Sahara by stressing the close ties between Spain and Morocco. Ironically, Istiql's leadership employed the same language of "Spanish-Moroccan brotherhood" that the Franco dictatorship had traditionally used for its own, albeit very different, purposes.[13]

The trajectory of Moroccan native Muhammed ben Mezzian Bel-Kassem, a friend and colleague in arms of Franco who rose to the rank of lieutenant general in the Spanish (sic) army, illustrates the ambiguities of Madrid's position most stunningly. Serving as the Spanish Captain-General of the Canary Islands in 1956, he became a marshal in the Moroccan armed forces after Moroccan independence that year. Given the proximity of the Canary Islands and its importance as a staging area for the impending Ifni War, Bel-Kassem thus came uncomfortably close to serving both sides in the same conflict. As the Spanish Captain-General after Moroccan independence, he did not—for obvious reasons—have open lines of communication with the governor of Spanish West Africa or direct responsibility for Ifni. In any case, Bel-Kassem soon made an abrupt jump from the Spanish army back to his native homeland. Indeed, his participation in the spring of 1958 as a representative of Morocco in Spain's handover of the Tarfaya Strip raised more than a few eyebrows among his Spanish former colleagues.[14]

After the Ifni War and the ceding of the Tarfaya Strip, the Madrid government stated unequivocally its intentions to hold on to the Sidi Ifni enclave and the entire Spanish Sahara, designating the two territories (along with Equatorial Guinea) as provinces of Spain. In fact, Madrid hoped that its recognition of Morocco's right to the southern zone of the protectorate (the Tarfaya Strip) would buy time and assuage Istiql´s annexationist tendencies. On the other hand, the designation of Ifni and the Sahara as Spanish provinces went along with a hard-line diplomatic stance that would prove increasingly untenable in an era of decolonization.[15] It was followed by a noticeable rise in Spanish colonization, investment, and development in the Sahara.[16] A decade later, Spain ceded Ifni to Morocco in the January 1969 Treaty of Fez. In return, Spain was guaranteed special fishing privileges over the next decade, although Morocco unilaterally abrogated this part of the treaty 3 years later.[17]

In the meantime, Sahrawi nationalism slowly became a force to be reckoned with. Spain, as the initial target of the nationalists' ire, responded somewhat ineptly to the new situation. Spanish authorities eventually moved toward granting more rights and political representation in the Sahara and Madrid, but these efforts came half-heartedly and late. In 1967, Spain created a new Jama'a (Djemma), or General Assembly of the Sahara, which was supposed to represent Sahrawi interests. In fact, however, its membership included many tribal leaders who collaborated with Spanish authorities. As a result, the body would have little credibility among many Sahrawis, especially the younger nationalists.[18] The situation foreshadowed Morocco's practice today of providing large financial incentives to collaborators, whose standing in turn diminishes in the ranks of the average Sahrawi.

Spain's inadequate response to the situation is not surprising; after all, under the Franco dictatorship, Spain itself lacked many political freedoms, so it is difficult to imagine that it would have implemented representative government anywhere else. Indeed, the ability of authoritarian governments to implement meaningful regional autonomy plans is open to question, as critics of Morocco's latest autonomy proposal for Western Sahara have pointed out.[19]

Although Western Sahara's days as a Spanish province were clearly numbered, many Spaniards still argue that had the Franco government acted differently, it might have prevented Morocco from occupying the territory in 1975. In fact, Spanish missteps at various levels helped set the stage for the current problems. A better understanding by the military high command of basic cultural, social, and political realities of indigenous societies would have helped. In particular, the Spaniards failed to pay sufficient attention to and adequately understand the most numerous and influential tribal confederation, the Rgaybat al-Sharq, and ignorant military policies inadvertently insulted and alienated many Sahrawis. Moreover, the Spanish persistence in ruling through traditional, older tribal elites became increasingly problematic, especially as those elites lost credibility among the younger generation.[20] Nevertheless, the petitions of the early nationalists were relatively moderate.

Demonstrating Spain's inability to comprehend and manage the evolving situation, a poorly attended public demonstration sponsored by Spanish agents and sheiks from the Jama'a was overshadowed by what would go down in Western Saharan history as the "Zamlah massacre" of June 1970, when security forces opened fire on a Sahrawi demonstration in El

Aaiún. Even though no Spaniards lost their lives, Spanish authorities responded harshly to the Zamlah upheaval: the first Sahrawi activist to press publicly for independence, Mohammed Sidi Ibrahim Bassiri, "disappeared" while in the custody of the Spanish military. The death of Bassiri was not only a tragedy, but also counterproductive for Spain. According to a leading historian of Western Sahara who was formerly a Spanish army intelligence officer there, Bassiri had not been a "revolutionary agitator, but rather a peaceful theorist of Arab liberation," and thus might have been brought into the Spanish camp.[21]

During this period of increasing tension in the Sahara, the Spaniards lacked a coherent national stance on the diplomatic stage. While the Spanish representation in the UN publicly revealed willingness to compromise, the Ministry of Foreign Affairs and office of the presidency sent mixed signals.[22] The latter, under Franco's close friend and confidant Admiral Luis Carrero Blanco, could at times reveal considerable ignorance and an utter inability to comprehend the exigencies of international diplomacy in an age of decolonization. When, for example, two Communist delegates in the United Nations (UN) questioned Spanish sovereignty over the Canary Islands, Carrero Blanco's hard-line camp responded with accusations of a "judeo-communist plot."[23]

In the meantime, Morocco had created the Ministry of Mauritanian and Saharan Affairs in 1965, charged with working toward the goal of Greater Morocco. Although Sahrawi nationalists now view Morocco as their primary foe, many logically saw the Spanish occupiers as their principal opponents before 1975. In 1971, El-Ouali Mustapha Sayed founded the Frente Popular para la Liberación de Saguia el-Hamra y Río de Oro (*Frente POLISARIO*, or Polisario Front), which explicitly called for armed struggle. In its very early days, the Polisario remained ambiguous about its grand strategic goal, and integration with Morocco or Mauritania did not appear totally out of the question. With the support of Libya, Algeria, and Mauritania, its forces began to attack Spanish interests, beginning with assaults on relatively small military outposts. On the international scene, the Polisario succeeded in bringing attention to its cause in the UN and elsewhere, but its leadership was slow to recognize the threat Morocco posed to its ultimate goal of independence.

In 1975, the situation finally came to a head. In May, a UN mission to Spanish Sahara encountered dramatic manifestations of public support for the Polisario and opposition to unification with Morocco or Mauritania, and on October 15, it issued a report in favor of Sahrawi self-determination. The next day, the International Court of Justice in The Hague made public its ruling against Morocco's claim to the territory, although Moroccan King Hassan II interpreted it otherwise. On the same day as the ruling, Hassan II announced what would become known as the "Green March," in which about 350,000 unarmed people were to walk across the border from Morocco into Western Sahara and claim it for the former. (Green is the traditional color of Islam). With this announcement, the king garnered tremendous domestic support from across the political spectrum, and volunteers for the march overwhelmed the recruiting offices that promptly opened throughout Morocco.

Spanish dictator Franco, in the meantime, was on his deathbed and under pressure from the United States and France to come to an agreement with Morocco and relinquish the Saharan territory. On October 30, the Moroccan volunteers for the Green March converged on Tarfaya, awaiting word from Hassan II to move into the Spanish Sahara (soon to be known as the Western Sahara or, to Morocco, as the "Southern Provinces"). On November 6, the volunteers crossed the border. Spanish soldiers received orders not to fire on the marchers, and they even assisted the marchers in avoiding landmines, although there was some fighting to the east between Moroccans and the Polisario forces who had occupied the recently withdrawn Spanish positions. Three days later, after Spain agreed to enter into negotiations for relinquishing the Sahara, Hassan II announced that the marchers could return to Tarfaya. On November 14, representatives from Spain, Morocco, and Mauritania signed the Pact of Madrid, which divided the territory between the two African countries. Franco, in the hospital and having been operated on twice since the Green March began, died early in the morning of November 20. Spain would formally complete its withdrawal from Western Sahara in February 1976.

Although rarely reflected in official Spanish government policies, the Polisario's cause enjoys a remarkable degree of popular support in Spain today. This support, which extends from leftist political activists to conservative military officers, translates into tangible benefits — economic and otherwise — for many Sahrawis, as we will see. It stems in no small part from a collective perception of guilt over the developments of 1975 and a belief that Spain could have decisively altered the course of events. According to this line of reasoning, the previous failure of Spanish colonial officials to manage Sahrawi nationalism before it became uncontrollable, combined with the subsequent

14

inability of hardliners in Madrid to recognize that decolonization was unavoidable, worked to the benefit of Hassan II. In other words, had the Spaniards played their cards differently, Western Sahara could arguably have achieved independence on terms beneficial to Spain while also precluding annexation by Morocco and Mauritania. Instead, key figures in Madrid, most notably Admiral Carrero Blanco, continued to insist that Spain would never relinquish the territory.

A more improbable counterfactual argument, especially popular among conspiracy theorists, maintains that the assassination of Carrero Blanco in late 1973, followed by Franco's long illness, left Spain without the kind of strong leadership that would have prevented the "betrayal" of the Sahrawis to Moroccan, French, U.S., and other outside interests. In fact, the United States appears to have pressured Spain on the issue and to have contributed, along with a Saudi-sponsored Strategic Studies group in London, to the planning of the Green March. General Vernon Walters, whose connections with the Moroccan monarchy went back decades, may have played a particularly significant role in the events, which Secretary of State Henry Kissinger also deemed important to U.S. interests in the region.[24] Kissinger feared a possible rise of Communist influence in the region.

Yet, regardless of any possible outside involvement by the United States, France, or anyone else, Spanish society was by no means willing to support a war with Morocco over the Sahara. Furthermore, it is not likely that the Spanish government, under a healthy Franco or anyone else, would have employed force to halt the Green March, especially when under strong pressure from the United States and elsewhere to avoid military conflict with Morocco. Spanish soldiers firing

15

upon masses of unarmed Moroccans would have provoked international outrage. Spain would also have suffered economic and diplomatic reprisals from Arab countries and in the Middle East, which had been a linchpin of Spanish international relations since World War II.

As the Spaniards withdrew, the Polisario occupied some of their positions and attacked the Moroccan and Mauritanian forces. According to witnesses, the Moroccan soldiers acted brutally as they invaded. As word spread of widespread murder, rape, and other atrocities, Sahrawi civilians, whom the Polisario had initially instructed to stay put, began to flee in mass.[25] During December 1975 and January 1976, some 40,000 people fled to refugee camps in the interior of the Sahara. The refugees consisted largely of women, children, and the elderly, as most of the men joined the Polisario military force. Moroccan planes subsequently launched air attacks on Sahrawi refugee camps, which caused hundreds of deaths, in some cases dropping napalm, white phosphorous, and fragmentation bombs.[26] Their intention was to force the refugees to return to the areas they had fled, now under Moroccan control. Instead, the bombings were counterproductive and, with them, the Moroccans squandered any possibility they might have had of winning over the Sahrawis. Moreover, the invasion and exodus helped break down traditional tribal barriers, facilitating the growth of Sahrawi national identity among the refugees now living together in the camps.[27]

In February 1976, as Spain officially ended its presence in Western Sahara, the Polisario proclaimed the Sahrawi Arab Democratic Republic (SADR), and its forces continued to launch effective guerrilla attacks on supply lines and economic and military targets. Seriously weakened by the war, the Mauritanian government withdrew its forces in 1979 and even recognized the SADR, much to the displeasure of Rabat. Not surprisingly, Morocco quickly claimed and annexed the area Mauritania had occupied, while the war between Morocco and the Polisario Front continued. With military aid from Algeria, Libya, and reportedly Cuba and North Korea on occasion, the Polisario Front posed a considerable challenge to the Moroccan armed forces throughout the war, even though the Moroccans benefited from very large amounts of aid from the United States and additional assistance from France, Saudi Arabia, and many other countries.[28] After adopting a defensive military strategy based on the enormous defensive barrier lines known as "the Wall" or "the Berm," Morocco succeeded in occupying about 80 percent of the disputed territory by 1991. But the FAR were unable to defeat the Polisario decisively; to do so would require invading Algeria, which continues to host enormous Sahrawi refugee camps. In 1991, a UN-supported ceasefire went into effect.

With the ceasefire, the UN assumed an active role in trying to bring about peace, but Morocco's resistance to a referendum and the Polisario's goal of complete independence impeded efforts at a resolution. In 1997, the UN appointed James Baker as special envoy for Western Sahara, and his efforts produced the only signed agreement between Morocco and Polisario: the Houston Agreement of September 1997. Baker continued his efforts to reach a solution until 2003, when he resigned in frustration over the intransigence of Morocco, which enjoyed considerable support from Washington after the terror attacks of 9/11. Since 2005, Sahrawi nationalists have employed "intifada" tactics in the Moroccan-occupied territories, while increasing dissatisfaction in the refugee camps around Tindouf, Algeria, is clear, especially among the younger generation. As we will see, there is also much fear that the influence of al-Qaeda in the Islamic Maghreb (AQIM) and other potential sources of instability in the Sahel may be spilling over into the refugee camps and the Western Sahara.

THE ROLE OF GEOGRAPHY

Terrain.

One cannot understand the Polisario insurgency's socio-cultural roots, military achievements, or the reason both sides eventually settled on a ceasefire without a good grasp of Western Saharan physical and human geography—neither of which has remained static. In fact, changes in both created the conditions for the insurgency and enabled it to develop so successfully. At the same time, Morocco's slowly learned ability to respond to and alter geographical conditions helped bring about the ceasefire of 1991, even though Morocco's actions also made a long-term solution more elusive in some ways.

As we have seen, northern Western Sahara is especially amenable to guerrilla activities, offering ample cover and good areas for small bases to those who know the terrain well. Yet, the southern portion of the territory has also proved difficult for counterinsurgency efforts. Making good use of their knowledge of the terrain, insurgents took advantage of the vast amount of space and their enemies' somewhat limited resources and unfamiliarity with the environment. During the colonial period, when the Spaniards and French began to employ air policing, the insurgents soon learned to avoid aerial detection by operating at night. Decades earlier, when the Polisario Front became active in the area, nocturnal operations still proved effective. During the 1980s, some observers believed that Moroccan acquisition of infrared technology would be disastrous for the Polisario. During this period, Morocco also installed Westinghouse radar systems and other electronic detection equipment from France and the United States, which provided Morocco with intelligence.[29]

Yet, terrain continued to favor the insurgents, in spite of any new technological superiority on the part of the Moroccans. Just as air power alone did not do the trick for the French and the Spaniards, radar and electronic sensors during the 1980s did not make a decisive difference in the Moroccan counterinsurgency campaigns against the Polisario: possibly because of an inability to buy sufficient infrared technology; poor training; or because the devices could not withstand high heat or effectively penetrate large-particle haze. The Moroccan military also lacked enough radar to cover all of its remote outposts.[30] As these constraints and the ineffectiveness of search-and-destroy tactics became clear, Morocco limited its focus to the "useful triangle" in the north, formed by the population centers of El Aaiún and Smara and the phosphate mines at Bukra', and then developed the defensive strategy of the Berm. Thus, only after adopting a new strategy, resting on this sophisticated and expensive system of walls, did the technological and materiel superiority of the Moroccan forces begin to overcome the geographical advantages formerly enjoyed by the Polisario forces. Even then, however, the Moroccans could only control the insurgency rather than defeat it definitively.

Natural Resources.

The natural resources in Western Sahara have shaped human geography, outside interests, and insurgent movements in several ways. Although it is incorrect to attribute Morocco's expansion into Western Sahara solely to the mineral resources there, Morocco clearly stands to gain from their full exploitation. The desire to develop the economic potential offered by Western Saharan geography began to grow in earnest after the discovery of large phosphate deposits by the Spaniards after World War II. Phosphate is a limited resource that is crucial to modern industrial agriculture, and the global demand for it is growing as its price continues to rise. Indeed, phosphate will be probably be instrumental for further agricultural development in India, sub-Saharan Africa, and many other parts of the world.

Madrid placed high hopes in reaping economic gains by exploiting the phosphate deposits at Bukra', which were discovered by a Spanish geologist in 1947. But it was not until 1972 that extraction and exportation began via the world's longest conveyor belt, stretching well over 100 km to the port of El Aaiún. Spanish military officials had recommended the construction of a railroad line instead of the conveyer belt, which was divided into sections between 7 and 11 km each, because they believed the belt would be too vulnerable. Predictably enough, in October 1974, a Polisario commando unit comprised of seven men and assisted by local workers rendered the conveyor belt inoperable.[31] Resuming operations after the Spanish withdrawal in late-1975, Bukra' and the conveyor belt have been primary objects of both Polisario attacks and Moroccan defensive strategy ever since.

Leading scholars of Western Sahara describe the phosphate reserves at Bukra' as "of an extremely high quality," noting that they are close to the surface. But they also write that at first the phosphates cost Morocco more than they were worth, pointing to the expenses incurred guarding the mine and conveyor belt and the steep drop in phosphate prices in the late-1970s.[32] Some officials at the Bukra' mine, moreover, depict the phosphates there as of poor quality and claim that the extraction is not cost-effective for Morocco, implying that the country's interest in Western Sahara's phosphate production stems from a political desire to demonstrate Morocco's economic commitment to the region.[33]

Yet, even if this claim was true, there is no question that Morocco, which is already the world's largest exporter of phosphates, understands well the significance of the substance to the country's current and future economic condition, and the country may be earning between $80 and $150 million each year from Bukra' alone. Recent debates about "peak phosphate theory" only highlight the future importance of this resource on the world stage.[34] According to one analysis, U.S. phosphate supplies will run out within the next 4 decades, but Morocco has a supply of at least 300 years, and other predictions about Morocco's ability to control the world market are even more dramatic. Without phosphate, global food production would decrease, contributing to possible famines in poor countries. Indeed, the issue has the potential to alter current appraisals of American strategic interests in the region. Theoretically, the United States and others might benefit from Western Saharan independence because the market position power in phosphate production of Morocco, which may be 85 percent of the world's phosphate reserves (including Western Sahara), would then decline.[35]

At present, however, fishing off of the Western Saharan coast probably has more immediate economic significance than phosphate production. Fishing has brought in millions, possibly billions, of dollars directly and indirectly, the latter through contracts with the European Union (EU) and other countries. [36] The Polisario has strongly contested Morocco's right to control these waters, at times acting with force against fishing boats from Spain and elsewhere that have entered them. Yet, in spite of these actions, the UN's position on the issue, and the Polisario's protests, the EU made agreements with Morocco over Western Saharan waters, even as the United States resisted negotiating with Morocco over the waters of the disputed territory.[37] In addition, outside fishing concerns reportedly bribe Moroccan officials in order to fish off the Saharan coast, resulting in destructive overfishing.[38]

The perceived potential of another natural resource, hydrocarbons, has attracted attention in Western Sahara since the Spanish period. Morocco, which spends heavily on oil imports, has a logical interest in any oil that may be there, as do major consuming countries worldwide. The United States, for instance, has revealed a growing inclination to look to Western Africa for oil, as Washington's willingness to ignore the many unpleasant aspects of the regime of another former Spanish colony, Equatorial Guinea, attests. Although Madrid made deals for oil surveying and exploration in the Sahara by foreign companies, these agreements failed to yield practical economic benefits, and since the Spanish withdrawal, the contentious situation has scared away potential investors. On this issue, the Polisario has done effective public relations work, and activists have convinced an American oil company to withdraw from an agreement it made with Morocco.[39] The Atlantic coast also figures into Algeria's geostrategic interests in establishing a friendly port there, thereby encircling Morocco. Although the establishment of the port is not a primary cause of the various actors' actions, it has served to fuel diplomatic and military alliances with the Polisario.

Two other exports from the Western Sahara are sand and salt. According to figures proved by the pro-Sahrawi organization Committee for the Protection of the Natural Resources of the Western Sahara (CSPRON) in 2009, 9.4 million tons of sand and 2,200 tons of salt are exported annually from the Western Sahara by Morocco.[40]

Human Geography.

As Zunes and Mundy note, if Western Sahara were to gain independence, it would be one of the least populated countries in the world. In 2000, the UN counted about 86,000 native Western Saharans of voting age. If the actual total is more than double this figure, Western Sahara still has one of the lowest population densities on the planet. The other half, living in "occupied territory" under Moroccan control, now constitutes a minority population, as Moroccan settlers and soldiers outnumber the indigenous population. Almost one half of the native population has lived as refugees in Algeria since 1976. According to a December 2008 report by Human Rights Watch, the camps near Tindouf are home to about 125,000 people.[41]

Yet, numbers alone do not tell the story. Nomadic traditions mean that common Western and even North African conceptions of boundaries, property, and government jurisdiction have historically had somewhat limited applicability in Western Sahara. Moreover, several special characteristics of the indigenous people—whose "national" identity is a recent development and a matter of some dispute—bear mention. The term *Sahrawi* as a term for the indigenous people of the Spanish Sahara came into being only in the mid-20th century, and some scholars and many Moroccans portray Sahrawi identity as a wholly artificial invention.[42]

Complicated questions of ethnicity, history, and cultural traditions make generalizations about Sahrawis difficult. Since the colonial period, outside observers have characterized Western Saharan society as "tribal"—with the tribes subdivided into fractions, subfractions, and families, with complex and sometimes overlapping alliances and rivalries. Sahrawis have been categorized in terms of castes, *cabilas*, and tribes, falling under such designations as "Arab Hassan" (descendants of the Arabs and warriors); "shurafa'" (descendants of the prophet); "Zawaya" (people of the Koran, or "scholarly"); "Zenagah" Berbers ("Sanhajah" in Arabic—associated with pastoral lifestyles and fishing); or "Tiknah" (assorted tribes from Northern Sahara and the Tarfaya region). Such categorization, however, implies a neatness and static quality to the designations, but the so-called castes and tribes and their respective characteristics can be dynamic and overlap.[43] On the other hand, tribal identities and interethnic relationships have undeniably shaped many aspects of Western Saharan history, and their social and political relevance, however diminished, persists.

Historically, the success or failure of Spanish occupational policies in the region often hinged on the understanding by military leaders of local ethnic identities and historical traditions. The relatively smooth occupation in 1934 of the Ifni area by Spain stemmed, in no small part, from Colonel Osvaldo Capaz's exceptional understanding of the local leadership, society, and culture. The Ifni region lies to the north of the current northern border of Western Sahara. But as Capaz knew well, in spite of their proximity, the peoples of Ifni tended to be more sedentary than the nomadic peoples of Spanish Sahara, with correspondingly different conceptions of property and jurisdiction, and he adjusted his dealings with local leaders accordingly. Conversely, subsequent Spanish military administrators in Western Sahara did not have Capaz's grasp of the tribal and social organizations. Because of their lack of knowledge, especially about the most important groupings in the territory—the Rgaybat confederations—they made policy errors that played tangible roles in the weakening of Spanish authority and the less-than-ideal circumstances of Spain's withdrawal from the Sahara 4 decades later.[44]

The native inhabitants of Western Sahara share many similarities with the Arab and Imazighen (Berber) ethnic groups of North Africa, and for many Moroccans, differences between themselves and the Sahrawis are not sufficient to deprive the latter of a Moroccan identity. For example, although nomadism traditionally characterized many tribes of the Spanish Sahara region, parts of Morocco also have strong nomadic traditions. Modern Sahrawi nationalism, however, emphasizes the linguistic, cultural, and nomadic characteristics and traditions that the nationalism believes uniquely unite all Sahrawis and distinguish them from others — especially Moroccans. At the same time, the Polisario negates — and actively suppresses — traditional tribal distinctions and hierarchies within the Western Sahara.

As is often the case, language reflects and fosters sentiments of national identity. Not only do the Sahrawis favor Hassaniya Arabic over Moroccan Arabic, or *Darija*, but when speaking a European tongue, they make a point of favoring Spanish over French, which they associate with Morocco. In fact, modern Sahrawi national identity also has a Hispanic component stemming from Spanish colonial history and more recent ties with Cuba.[45] Curiously, Spanish colonization also fostered the spread of Hassaniya. After Spain began colonizing the Ifni region in 1934, relations between Ifni's Ba Amrani and neighboring peoples increased. With time, the use of Hussaniya in Ba Amrani Cabilas, whose native language was the Berber dialect of Tassasit, increased markedly.[46] Along the same lines, today's second generation "settlers" from Morocco to Western Sahara often speak Hassaniya.[47]

It is clear that language is a fundamental aspect of Sahrawi national identity, as reflected in perhaps the most useful definition of Sahrawis — "the Hassaniyyah-speaking peoples who claim membership among at least one of the social groupings found in and around the area now known as Western Sahara."[48] But even this definition is not perfect, as its authors write. The Moroccan government's policy of moving people into the Sahara — thereby deliberately altering the region's traditional human geography — has further confused the matter. Among the Moroccan settlers in Western Sahara are many ethnic Sahrawis from southern Morocco. Even when they share the same language and social systems as those of the Sahrawis from Western

Sahara, their overall political allegiance or sense of national identity may differ.

Needless to say, this lack of agreement on the fundamental question of what constitutes a Sahrawi only further complicates the efforts of the UN and others to find reliable census figures or organize a plebiscite, and Morocco's tendency to obfuscate the issue to its own advantage does not help. Furthermore, the varying degrees of collaboration between many Sahrawis and Moroccan authorities over the years cannot be erased, creating paradoxical mixes of political and ethnic identities. Should the Polisario ever achieve its goal of full independence, the ensuing "settling of accounts" with collaborators will be ugly and may well lead to civil war, as Sahrawis who have recognized and benefited from Moroccan sovereignty fear.[49]

Climate, Politics, and Changes in Human Geography.

Spain's attempts to exploit natural resources and its policies of economic development, however modest compared with Cold War-era U.S. modernization projects, increased the tendency among the traditionally nomadic peoples of the Sahara to adopt more sedentary lifestyles. In the meantime, several droughts since the mid-1950s also contributed to a decline in the nomadic way of life among Sahrawis. The generally unfavorable climate between 1956 and 1969 led to a big drop in the animal population, which helps explain why the Polisario military relied so heavily on Land Rovers rather than on the traditional Sahrawi military use of camels.[50]

Until the Spanish withdrew in 1975, the consequences of increased sedentariness and economic development, however limited, were multifold. First, the nationalist, anti-Spanish, and then anti-Moroccan ideologies spread faster and easier in places with more sedentary populations than among the dispersed and ambulant tribes of the desert.[51] The increased awareness and exploitation of natural resources also stimulated resentment against outsiders for profiting while Sahrawis remained at the bottom of the economic hierarchy. Moreover, sedentariness seems to have brought with it an increased demand for consumer goods and growing unhappiness with the current situation, just as international anti-colonial and pan-Arab rhetoric found more receptive listeners, especially among the younger generation. In the meantime, the economic potential of natural resources only further attracted the attention of Rabat, where Western Sahara already had a prominent place in the nationalist vision of "Greater Morocco" and the Alawi dynasty's legitimacy. During the Spanish period, Morocco thus had an interest in stimulating anti-colonial resistance among Sahrawis, although such Sahrawi nationalist resistance would eventually stand in the way of Rabat's own annexationist objectives over the long term.

IDEOLOGIES AND ORGANIZATIONS

The strength of the ideologies of the principal protagonists of Western Sahara conflict helps explain why it has lasted so long. At the time of Moroccan independence, the father of Moroccan nationalism and head of the Istiql party Allal al-Fassi published his map of "Greater Morocco," the establishment of which became an explicit goal of the Moroccan monarchy. Going back to the 11th century, he argued that Morocco's historical borders encompassed a very large portion of northwestern Africa, including significant chunks of Algeria and Mali and all of Western Sahara and Mauritania, extending southward to the Senegal River. In October 1957, the new Moroccan state officially adopted the ideology of Greater Morocco, and the `Alawi dynasty staked its legitimacy in part on the preservation of its "southern provinces," as it calls the Western Sahara. As a component of Moroccan national identity, the belief that Western Sahara belongs to Morocco has enjoyed widespread domestic support. The monarchy, subjected at various times to assassination attempts, food riots, and other threats, has not shied away from appealing to this aspect of Moroccan nationalism, especially in times of crisis. [52]

The Polisario Front's ideology makes similar use of the powerful force of nationalism, building upon fundamental notions of sovereignty, anti-colonialism, and Sahrawi national identity. As we have seen, Sahrawi national identity is largely (if not entirely) a modern invention, and Spanish colonialism played a key role in the inception and development of nationalism in Western Sahara. Yet, even if it appears artificial and lacks deep historical roots, Sahrawi nationalism has exhibited remarkable effectiveness as a galvanizing force for the Polisario insurgency. One can argue, moreover, that all nationalisms are "artificial" entities serving political interests. In any case, the actions of Spain, and especially of Morocco beginning in 1975, did much to bring the peoples of Western Sahara together in the face of a perceived common threat. As refugees together endured bombings by the Moroccan Air Force and other hardships, traditional tribal distinctions diminished, fostering perceptions of community and shared identity.

Nevertheless, the Polisario's achievements resulted from far more than the force of Sahrawi national identity alone, invented or otherwise. Along with nationalist sentiments, the organization of the movement and its modern socio-cultural outlook also explain its success. The Polisario was founded with a program that strongly reflected the influence of the Arab liberation movement, exemplified by Egypt's Nasser, Algeria's Bumedian, and Libya's Quaddafi. It is not surprising, then, that the Polisario's struggle has been categorized as a revolutionary insurgency.[53] In the era of the Cold War, such a program did not exactly facilitate sympathy for its cause by Western countries.

Yet, the Polisario leadership learned to downplay its initial Socialist and pan-Arab program, even as it relied on the support of countries like Algeria and Libya. According to one of its historical leaders, the Polisario "was always a nationalist movement, not a Marxist movement. There were always Marxists in the Polisario, but also many other tendencies."[54] Indeed, in practical terms, the movement's most revolutionary aspects lie less in Marxist economics than in the cultural front, exemplified by: its rejection of traditional tribal affiliations and hierarchies; its prioritization of education; abolishment of slavery; and, support for women's rights. Tellingly, the Polisario Front has managed to garner some of its strongest outside political and diplomatic support from Spanish conservatives like the strongly pro-American former president José María Aznar (1996-2004), who lent more practical diplomatic and moral assistance to the Polisario than did his Socialist predecessors or successors. The conservative support for the Polisario comes from a complex mix of traditional Spanish paternalist colonial ideology, feelings of guilt over the "betrayal" of the

Sahrawis in 1975, and the good relations that sometimes formed among Spanish and Sahrawi comrades in arms. In February 1976, when the Polisario proclaimed the SADR, it presented the new state as free, independent, sovereign, ruled by a system of national democracy, and Islamic. The Polisario's spokesman described the state as desirous of peace but fighting to defend its independence, territorial integrity, and natural resources and wealth.[55]

The Polisario looked to existing Socialist regimes of the era when setting up its political organization, and it used Vietnamese and Algerian models for its military structure.[56] Organizationally, the Polisario consisted of three wings: the political wing for propaganda and psychological operations; the diplomatic wing; and the military wing, initially tasked with undertaking actions against Spanish forces. The principal figure was the Secretary General who was assisted by an executive committee of nine members. Those nine members were also among the 21 members of the executive wing. Three members of the executive wing had specific responsibility for "mass organizations," including three social categories: workers, peasants, and women. The political bureau members elected 19 members of the "people's committees" to serve as the "people's national council." At the base of the organization, every group of 10 people constitutes a cell, and each faction/band ("bando") had its own military and political hierarchy.[57]

INSURGENCY AND COUNTERINSURGENCY: MILITARY METHODS AND DEVELOPMENTS

In the wake of the Green March and Spain's announcement that it would withdraw its forces from the Sahara, the Polisario's future looked bleak to many observers. The U.S. ambassador in Rabat believed that the desert terrain would facilitate a relatively smooth and rapid counterinsurgency campaign by Morocco, and an International Institute for Strategic Studies report made similar predictions.[58] After all, even the Spaniards, who had committed significant policy errors and disposed of relatively few resources, had managed to maintain a presence in the Sahara for nearly a century. Hence, in the eyes of many observers, Morocco should have been able to suppress the Sahrawi insurgency fairly easily.

Needless to say, the insurgency proved to be far more difficult to put down than anyone expected; a quarter of a century later, the conflict remains unresolved. Reasons for the Polisario's survival include its access to outside support and sanctuaries, international diplomacy and public relations, and some luck. Nevertheless, developments in the purely military sphere go far to explain why the early predictions of easy Moroccan success proved so wrong. The strategic and tactical thought of the Polisario's military leadership, the high level of morale and experience of its soldiers, and the Sahrawis' ability to use geography to their advantage proved more than a match for their opponents. On the other side, the Mauritanian armed forces disposed of relatively few human and materiel resources, while the ineffectiveness and operational shortcomings of Moroccan counterinsurgency (COIN) manifested itself on various occasions.

Long before the Polisario war, the success of Spain's military in the initial conquest and long occupation of the Sahara stemmed from various factors, including the relatively peaceful nature and isolated situation of the first indigenous contacts, the skills and experience of key Spanish military leaders, and the lack of negative outside interference or sanctuaries. In fact, it suited France, as the leading outside power in the area, for the tribes of Spanish Sahara to be submitted to colonial control. Moreover, the nomadic character and low numbers of the indigenous tribes helped keep them from posing a significant threat to authorities.

When troubles arose most notably in the Ifni War, they came as much from outside as from within the territory: namely, from the newly independent state of Morocco. On the battlefield, the Spaniards' learning curve was steep, and it took considerable efforts to overcome Spanish shortcomings in military planning, logistics, and command and control issues. Spanish COIN was more noteworthy in the ensuing cleanup of LA forces in the Sahara. Benefiting from the experience of the successful airborne drops during the Ifni War, the Spanish military made extensive and very effective use of columns of paratroopers to attack LA forces and relieve besieged garrisons in the Sahara. Of course, Operation HURRICANE was also a joint enterprise, in which the participation of the French was crucial. [59]

By the time the Spaniards left, Western Sahara had changed dramatically, experiencing a significant decline in nomadism, a corresponding growth of urban areas, and increased economic development. Thus, while the efficacy of Spanish military methods explain, in part, the longevity of Spain's rule, it is equally true that after 1975, the Sahrawis gained the capability to mount military and political attacks of a scale and sophistication that the Spaniards had rarely, if ever, faced. Moreover, Sahrawi nationalism had exploded into a formidable force. Thus, while contrasting the relative success of Spanish civil affairs and political COIN in North Africa with that of its Moroccan counterpart may have some value, a contrast between the purely military methods of Spanish and Moroccan counterinsurgency campaigns is less useful.

The Polisario Front vs. Morocco and Mauritania: 1975-79.

As Morocco's FAR moved rapidly across Western Sahara after the Green March of November 1975, thousands of Sahrawi men, many with relevant experience and training from their service in the Spanish armed forces, joined the Polisario Front's military wing. In some cases, moreover, Spanish soldiers may have donated arms and supplies as they departed.[60] Polisario forces soon took part in a nearly continuous series of guerrilla attacks against the FAR, which had employed large motorized columns to occupy positions deep into the Sahara by early-February 1976. On February 5, the Moroccans took Tifariti near the northern Mauritanian border, and a week later, they occupied Guelta to the southwest. Shortly thereafter, a column of five FAR battalions moved toward the Mahbes in the northeastern corner of the Western Sahara near the Moroccan and Algerian borders. Before doing so, the Moroccans sought and received assurances from Algeria that it would not oppose the occupation of Mahbes.[61]

The Polisario Front's military forces, known as the Sahrawi Popular Liberation Army (*Ejército de Liberación Popular Sahuraui*, or ELPS) responded to the FAR's rapid movements and occupations with surprising effectiveness. Beginning in 1976, the military forces benefited from an increase in the depth and breadth of their armaments and other supplies, which until this point had come solely from Algeria

34

and Libya. Now they received valuable weaponry from North Korea and elsewhere, and by 1978, the weapons at their disposal included recoilless artillery, 14.5 mm ZPU anti-aircraft machine guns, 120 mm mortars, multiple rocket launchers, SAM 7 portable missile launchers, and rocket-propelled grenades (RPGs). They would also acquire T-55 tanks, SAM 6 missile systems, armored troop carriers, and Soviet amphibious tracked infantry fighting vehicles (BMPs) and Soviet armored reconnaissance/surveillance vehicles (BTRs). Weapons mounted on pickup truck beds, as seen recently in combat in Libya, boosted the Polisario's offensive power.[62]

Even with such weaponry, however, the Polisario's military endeavors would not have met with so much success had the ELPS not perfected the tactics of desert insurgency, practiced earlier on a smaller scale against the Spanish military. To minimize the disadvantage of the lack of cover in the desert, the ELPS would create a large buffer zone between themselves and the Moroccan positions. From their own positions, they would suddenly attack Moroccan forces on the move and then quickly pull back. When the ELPS succeeded in dislodging the FAR from strong points, the guerrilla bands might temporarily occupy them but would then withdraw rapidly in order to attack again against other strong points. In this way, they subjected the Moroccan positions to continuous offensives, and their operational capacity continued to improve. Fighting was especially fierce during the summers, when the Sahrawis were better adapted to the hot climate than were the vast majority of the Moroccan soldiers.[63]

By April 1977, the ELPS had downed 18 planes and combat helicopters and two cargo planes, and taken out some 600 vehicles. According to some casualty figures, the FAR suffered 4,200 deaths, 2,800 wounded, and had 96 soldiers taken prisoner, while the Mauritanian forces had 1,600 deaths, 900 wounded, and 16 soldiers taken prisoner. One explanation for the ratios, if correct, may be that the ELPS made it a policy not to take prisoners.[64]

Yet, the Polisario's military feats, although a significant concern for Morocco, did not bring strategic victory, as they succeeded neither in destroying nor expelling the FAR. Not only were the Polisario forces much smaller than those of their enemies, but they were incapable of the kind of operational coordination that fighting the two powers in separate areas entailed.[65] As we will see, an inability to coordinate forces and actions over the large desert theater would continue to pose difficulties for both the ELPS and its opponents even after Mauritania withdrew from the war. In the meantime, it was difficult to discern much in Polisario strategic thought beyond the classic protracted war strategy. Overall, the Polisario insurgency, although not fitting neatly into the category of protracted revolutionary war, reveals the clear influence of Mao, and the victory of the National Liberation Front (FLN) over the French in Algeria was also a source of inspiration.[66] But ELPS leaders, made aware relatively early in the war that their many tactical triumphs were not leading to decisive victory, looked beyond the usual Maoist platitudes to focus on the peculiarities of their own situation. In particular, they took note of the unequal partnership of the countries they faced and made strategic adjustments accordingly.[67]

After first simply targeting exposed enemy forces wherever it found them, the ELPS leadership soon decided to attack its opponents in detail, albeit at a strategic rather than a tactical level. Shifting to a more reserved posture toward the FAR, the ELPS leaders began to direct the brunt of their offensives against Mauritania, which was clearly the weaker of their enemies. In this fashion, the Polisario leadership sought to compel Mauritania to drop out of the conflict, thereby leaving Morocco in a more vulnerable position.[68]

The targets of the ELPS would thus be as much economic and political as military; instead of simply trying to destroy the Mauritanian army, the Polisario aimed to weaken the government so much that it would have no choice but to seek peace. Yet, while the Polisario's strategic goals against Mauritania were political and economic, it relied almost exclusively on military methods to achieve them. At this point in the war, the role of diplomacy was relatively small.

In July 1976, a Polisario band made a 400-km journey to the suburbs of the Mauritanian capital, Nouakchott, and shelled it. On May 1, 1977, Polisario forces launched an audacious attack on the Mauritanian mining city of Zouerate. In this case, they went up against formidable defenses, including a garrison of 1,000 soldiers and a wall of more than 60 km. With a column of 60 light vehicles and some 300 men, they attacked the European quarter of the city, home to more than 700 French technical workers from the mine and their families. The attackers not only inflicted numerous casualties on the Mauritanian garrison, but they also took six French hostages. Because of resulting security concerns, foreign workers began to leave Mauritania, causing a major interruption of iron mining. This interruption, along with attacks on the Zouerate-

Nouadhibou railroad, seriously damaged the Mauritanian economy.[69] The Polisario followed up in July with another attack on Nouakchott, reached via a very long detour along the Algerian border so as to avoid contact with Mauritanian and Algerian forces. The ELPS forces, consisting of 600 men; over 100 vehicles; and ample arms, munitions, and supplies; reached Nouakchott, but suffered unexpected resistance and casualties at the hands of the Mauritanian military. More casualties resulted during their subsequent withdrawal from Mauritania.[70]

The Nouakchott operation had several important consequences. Above all, it represented another step toward the Polisario's longer-term strategic goal of undermining the Morocco-Mauritania alliance and precipitating regime change in Nouakchott, even though, in purely military terms, it largely failed. More immediately, as a result of Mauritania's protests after the attack, Algeria limited somewhat the Polisario's use of Algerian territory as a launching point for future offensives. Morocco also became more involved in the fighting in Mauritania, as it began to fear for the fate of its ally. Another consequence of the Nouakchott operation was the death during the fighting of El-Ouali Mustapha Sayed, the prestigious, charismatic Secretary General and the head of the Polisario's military wing. His death provoked an internal debate within the Polisario over the scope of military operations. The leadership subsequently decided to further intensify the military attacks, while also undertaking a major "national" program of political and social mobilization in the refugee camps.[71] The Polisario forces also experienced the consequences of targeting French interests, most dramatically outside Nouakchott, when they ran into recently arrived AML-10 armored vehicles from France. Nonetheless, the Polisario would continue to attack Zouerate and take French hostages. The French responded by becoming more involved in the conflict, making use of their military base in Dakar, Senegal. Their intervention continued until June 1978, when Mauritania's defeat was clear, and nearly all the French technicians had been evacuated.[72]

As the Polisario's offensives continued, Mauritania's problems increased. Although the Mauritanian armed forces were relatively small—numbering only about 18,000 men during the conflict—for a country of its population, the drain of mobilizing so many men was considerable. Mauritania received some financial assistance from Saudi Arabia, Kuwait, and the Ivory Coast, but in 1977, the costs of the war consumed around 40 percent of the national budget, and in 1978, that figure rose to 60 percent. Moreover, the war grew increasingly unpopular among the rank-and-file soldiers. For many of the black soldiers in the Mauritanian army, who made up a majority of the soldiers but were often regarded disparagingly by other Mauritanians, it was a war between Arabs in which they failed to perceive a real stake, while many soldiers of Arab and Berber origin did not understand why they had to fight an enemy with which they had long enjoyed close ties.[73] In the officer corps, there was resentment of the need to rely on Moroccan (and French) support to defend the country, which left Mauritanian commanders feeling insulted and with the sense that their authority had been challenged.[74]

During 1977, there were various changes in the Mauritanian cabinet and military commands, and in July 1978, there was a *coup d'état* in Nouakchott, to be followed by more governmental shifts in the months that followed. Tellingly, during these events, Mauritanian political leaders largely avoided references to the Polisario, instead emphasizing their desire to get the Moroccans out of their country.[75] After a year-long ceasefire and then a brief resumption of hostilities, the Polisario Front and Mauritania signed a peace agreement on August 5, 1979.

In the end, the Polisario's strategy had worked. Not only had the military attacks destabilized the Mauritanian state so much that it withdrew from the war, but the withdrawal left Morocco more vulnerable. The economic and military drain on Morocco was also clear; the FAR had grown from 60,000 men in 1975 to double that in 1979, the majority of whom were deployed in the Sahara.[76] Algeria, against whom Morocco had fought and lost a border dispute known as the Sand War in 1963, thus had less to worry about from its neighbor. Now, without its former Mauritanian ally, the FAR had to defend much more territory. As would soon become clear, moreover, the ELPS was in the position to launch attacks within Morocco proper.

The Continued Failure of Moroccan COIN: 1979-80.

After the Polisario-Mauritania peace treaty, Hassan II, whose government perceived Algerian pressure behind the negotiations, not only claimed the Western Saharan territory formerly occupied by Mauritania, but also stated that under no circumstances in the future would his country give up its right to the entire Sahara. By the same token, however, he had no intention of going to war with Algeria. The struggle against the Polisario had already significantly damaged the economy of Morocco. In 1979, military expenses reportedly made up some 40 percent of the state budget, although other estimates are lower, and generous loans from Saudi Arabia eased the financial burden.[77] In this situation, the FAR would prove inadequate to the task of suppressing the insurgency. The Polisario, in contrast, reached a high point in its effectiveness.

By 1978, the ELPS had more or less assumed the form of a conventional army; 2 years later, it probably numbered around 20,000 men, equipped with a diverse set of modern armaments and vehicles. With them, it could undertake far-reaching operations involving hundreds of vehicles and thousands of men. The ELPS soldiers made excellent use of their knowledge of the terrain—along with Soviet-armored BMPs and light, Land Rover-type vehicles—to achieve mobility and surprise. In addition to attacking Moroccan positions and military columns, the ELPS soldiers also targeted supply convoys with frequency, cut power supplies, and attacked the mines at Bukra', halting phosphate extraction for 6 months.[78]

In contrast, the FAR had significant deficiencies. Unlike the Sahrawis, soldiers from the Rif, the Atlas Mountains, and Morocco's towns and cities had a hard time adapting to the climate, which could be exceedingly hot during the day but then very cold at night. Because the logistical lines between Tan-Tan, Tarfaya, and El Aaiún were so vulnerable, many Moroccan positions did not receive supplies regularly. The FAR commanders displayed scant initiative, and some mid-level commands were incapable of undertaking operations at all.[79] Military orders came from the headquarters of Hassan II, who—after surviving assassination attempts in 1971 and 1972—preferred to keep tight control over the FAR. The Moroccan army made little use of COIN tactics, assuming instead a defensive posture in trenches around population centers or advanced positions. The FAR shunned attempts to seek out the ELPS bands that roamed the desert. These deficiencies help explain why the FAR would perform so poorly in the late-1970s and early-1980s, in spite of its indisputable material advantage.[80]

Well aware of Morocco's military weaknesses, the Polisario planned a sort of Sahrawi version of the Tet Offensive (albeit somewhat more spread out over time and probably not directly inspired by Vietnam.) The Huari Bumedian Offensive, named after the recently deceased Algerian president, was to be a general, systematic attack on FAR positions and economic targets in the Sahara and within Morocco (i.e., not just its southern provinces). The offensive aimed to inflict significant military and economic damage and undermine the credibility of the Moroccan government forces, thereby diminishing the capability and will of the country to remain in Western Sahara.[81] The offensive also served as a clear signal that Algeria would not waver in its support for the Polisario.[82]

The offensive began on January 1, 1979, and succeeded in bringing the Bukra' conveyor belt to a halt within days. In the middle of the month, there were more attacks north of El Aaiún. Then, on January 28, Polisario forces struck inside Morocco at Tan-Tan, the capital of Tarfaya. On the logistical line between Agadir and El Aaiún, the city hosted an air base and a garrison of several thousand Moroccan soldiers. The attackers managed to occupy the city for 4 hours, during which they freed 118 Sahrawi prisoners; took various Moroccans captive; and destroyed military installations, gasoline depots, and the electric power plant.[83]

As the Polisario intended, these offensives had serious repercussions in Morocco, where the public realized after the attack on Tan-Tan that the war was not going as well as the government claimed. Indeed, after the Polisario's brief but highly effective occupation of that city, Morocco's political parties demanded a parliamentary meeting to discuss the Sahara issue. By early March, the king publicly admitted that the situation was not getting better, and he announced the formation of a new national council on security comprised of a surprisingly wide range of the political spectrum. He also reorganized the FAR, replacing its commander for the southern provinces.[84]

Less than 2 weeks later, Polisario forces launched fierce attacks on the principal population centers in northern Western Sahara, and at the end of the month, they occupied Tifariti. In the meantime, they harassed the communication lines between Tan-Tan, Tarfaya, and El Aaiún so effectively that the latter henceforth had to be supplied by sea. After various other tactical successes, on August 24, a Polisario column scored a major victory against the Moroccan Third Armored Division near Leboirat. Caught by surprise, the Moroccans offered relatively little resistance, and many abandoned their posts and equipment. They suffered over 1,000 casualties and had more than 100 prisoners taken, whom the Polisario subsequently displayed — along with the materiel they had seized — before the international press. The division also lost 37 T-54 tanks in the encounter, and 77 Moroccan soldiers were subsequently charged with cowardice or negligence. At the strategic level, however, the Polisario failed in its objective for southern Morocco of bringing the FAR out of their footholds in Wadi al-Dhahab.[85]

In early-October, a column of over 5,000 men attacked Samara, a Saharan holy city defended by a Moroccan garrison of 6,000 soldiers. The attackers managed to penetrate the defensive parameter and free some 700 Sahrawi prisoners before Moroccan air attacks with F-1 Mirages forced the Polisario forces to withdraw. On their way back to bases in Algeria, the Polisario attacked and briefly occupied Mahbes, destroying Moroccan military installations there. In the wake of these successes, the Polisario leadership decided to intensify its attacks, including operations in Moroccan territory north of the Draa River and east of Tarfaya. In short, Morocco's predicament was becoming serious, and its military leaders believed that they would not be able to defeat the Polisario definitively without pursuing its forces into Algeria, which was not possible. For this reason, Morocco made a major strategic shift.[86]

Recognizing that the FAR could not attain control over a large amount of hostile territory, the Moroccans elected to withdraw from the smaller positions and fortifications that had not yet fallen to the enemy, limiting their forces to areas of Guelta and Bir Nzarán and within the so-called useful triangle of Bukra', Samara and El Aaiún, thereby focusing on a strategically important area of a relatively high population density and economic value. At the same time, the Moroccans formed well-armed and supplied motorized columns ("flying columns") meant for rapid, simultaneous operations in the unoccupied territories. The Moroccans also made at least some use of the traditional COIN technique of reconcentration, removing the Polisario-friendly civilian population from Saac in order to separate the insurgents from a source of support.[87]

U.S. Responses to Moroccan Military Losses and the Limitations of Moroccan Strategy.

As the position of its strategic ally Morocco became more precarious, the United States increased its military support. Morocco began to receive much larger amounts of foreign aid beginning in 1978, when the FAR appeared especially threatened by the Sahrawi insurgents. France and the United States supplied much of the materiel, while Saudi Arabia provided generous financing. The French also helped in the areas of training and intelligence, drawing from their previous experiences in the Sahara. In addition, Egypt, Iran under the Shah, Jordan, Libya, Iraq, South Africa, Belgium, Italy, Spain, and Brazil supplied arms to Morocco during the war with the Polisario.[88]

The Carter administration (1977-80) initially placed some restrictions on U.S. arms sales to Rabat, but these limitations dissipated after the Polisario's attacks inside Morocco and the fall of the Shah of Iran in 1979, as the White House now perceived a stronger need to strengthen its remaining strategic allies in the Middle East and Africa. During the Ronald Reagan presidency (1981-89), U.S. support for Morocco was especially strong. Indeed, the Reagan administration made it clear in a number of ways that it saw strategic value in aiding Morocco in its war against the Polisario. Joseph Reed, a friend of King Hassan, became the only noncareer U.S. ambassador in the Middle East. After Polisario forces with heavy armor and sophisticated weaponry inflicted a damaging attack at Galtah Zammur and brought down several Moroccan planes in October 1981, Central Intelligence Agency (CIA) director William Casey personally delivered a request for support from King Hassan to Reagan. Numerous meetings between U.S. diplomatic, military, and intelligence officials followed, including meetings in December between King Hassan and Secretary of Defense Caspar Weinberger and the Senate Foreign Relations Committee chair Charles Percy. In February, Secretary of State Alexander Haig met the Moroccan monarch, who met with Reagan the following May. Visits to Morocco by Vice President George H. W. Bush and then U.S. representative to the UN, Jeanne Kirkpatrick, both in September 1983, highlighted the continued importance of Morocco to U.S. policy.[89]

Between 1976 and 1984, the U.S. Government spent an average of $1 million per year in training officers in the Moroccan armed forces, including pilots and COIN specialists. By 1982, well over 100 U.S. military advisors were in Morocco, and many Moroccans received training on U.S. military bases. The U.S. Air Force trained Moroccan pilots in missile countermeasures, evasion, and other relevant techniques. In addition, the Moroccans received assistance in finding the positions of Polisario-operated SA-6s, although the FAR does not appear to have made effective use of this intelligence. A group of American advisors was also sent to train a battalion-sized unit to carry out special operations against Polisario SA-6 positions.[90]

At least through the early-1980s, however, the tactical and operational failings combined with flawed strategies to prevent Moroccan victory. It is likely that U.S., French, or other foreign advisors played a role in Morocco's decision to focus on the useful triangle or to employ the COIN-focused columns, the formation of which coincided with increasing U.S. military aid. The recognition of the useful triangle as a strategic center of gravity would eventually serve as the starting point for the development of a new strategy of static defense, but overall, the flying columns proved largely ineffective. Indeed, the FAR failed to cleanse the target areas' guerrilla activity, establish dominance over the Polisario forces, or even damage them significantly. Thus, the initiative remained with the Polisario.

At the operational and tactical levels, major shortcomings included the lack of flexibility in the levels of command below the king, which had become standard after the failed coups of the early-1970s. When a field commander under attack requested air support, he had to go through Rabat. The subsequent delay gave Polisario forces time to carry out raids and then withdraw before the power could be brought to bear. It is telling that the Royal Gendarmerie, which policed the military on the king's behalf, counted bullets before and after training exercises. Strategically, the Moroccans still attempted to hold too much territory. Although the size of the Moroccan army had increased dramatically, it could not effectively defend and supply as widely as its strategists had hoped, and the overextension made tactical weaknesses and logistical problems very apparent.[91] Thus, the initiative remained with the Polisario. Given the need to avoid open war with Algeria and the conditions in which it had to fight, the Moroccan armed forces were incapable of defeating such a determined enemy as the Polisario.

"The Berm": Success in Defensive Strategy?

After the failure of the attack columns, Morocco adopted a clear-and-hold strategy based on the construction of a series of well-defended barriers, or berms, known colloquially as "the Berm," "the Wall," or, to Polisario sympathizers, "the Wall of Shame."[92] Some analysts have strongly criticized this approach, noting that the walls have not proved impenetrable and that the new strategy of static defense was extremely costly and ceded the advantages of surprise, initiative, and audacity to the ELPS.[93] Indeed, the construction of the barriers represented a clear admission by Morocco that it had to accept "in the best case a long war of attrition or, in the worst case, total stalemate."[94] On the other hand, the barriers basically succeeded in keeping the insurgents out of the occupied territory, protected key interests, and allowed Morocco to establish civil administration in important parts of Western Sahara. With the completion of all 1,500 miles of barrier, Morocco would gain control of over 80 percent of Western Sahara, making the project "the largest functional military barrier in the world."[95] The wall has also facilitated the influx of thousands of Moroccan settlers into former Spanish Sahara.[96]

The construction of the walls, which began in 1981, proceeded in stages, with the final part completed in April 1987.[97] The early barriers aimed to protect the useful triangle area and the Moroccan garrison near Algeria from attacks from across the border. This meant that Morocco initially renounced control over much of the territory, especially in the south (not including the population centers of Dakhla and Aargub in the former Spanish bay of Río de Oro, where the FAR maintained significant garrisons). In 1983, work began on another phase in the Berm construction, employing some 30,000 Moroccan soldiers. Here the location of the new wall appears to have been largely political: by dividing the Sahara right at the corner border with Mauritania, Morocco may have endeavored to force the Polisario to tread on Mauritanian soil when launching attacks in the south, thereby implicating Mauritania in the conflict. Further Berm construction continued in southward pattern, eventually cutting the Polisario territory off from the Atlantic coast.[98]

The walls were constructed in a similar manner throughout: first, a bulldozer dug a trench, the sand or dirt from which was then used for an embankment of two or three meters in height; the walls were protected by mine fields, barbed wire, and electronic sensors, with posts scattered along their length and guarded by 100,000 to 170,000 soldiers. The soldiers were deployed either in frontal positions or in bases to the rear, armed with artillery and from which rapid reaction forces were to emerge if the wall were breached. Operationally, regional commanders enjoyed more autonomy than before, including the ability to call in and receive more timely support. Although relatively small penetrations were not difficult, large-scale attacks were more problematic. Once they had detected a breach, the FAR could block the entry point and then attack the trapped Polisario forces with ground and air power.[99]

To meet manpower requirements, the Moroccan government had to periodically authorize special volunteer recruitments and create many new units. Just the construction of the sixth wall, for instance, entailed personnel needs of between 10,000 and 15,000 men and the creation of a mechanized regiment, an airborne battalion, six infantry battalions, two artillery groups, a sapper battalion, and a transportation battalion. Even long after the declaration of the ceasefire in 1991, the Berm remains the largest minefield in the world; since 2006, the UN Mission for the Referendum in Western Sahara (MINURSO) has coordinated the removal of mines—a task in which both Morocco and the Polisario Front have pledged to assist.[100]

Once completed, the system of berms had a clear impact on the ELPS, which saw its room for tactical and operational maneuver shrink significantly. The combat that did take place was increasingly attritional in nature. In September 1983, for example, Polisario forces consisting of five mechanized battalions and two armored battalions with more than 50 tanks attacked the first wall near Samara along a 50-km front, and the ensuing battle acquired a markedly conventional character.[101]

In the meantime, developments on the diplomatic front had consequences on the battlefield. The August 1983 Treaty of Uxda between Morocco and Libya provoked a strong reaction from Algeria, which strongly criticized the "unnatural" nature of the agreement between the traditionalist Moroccan monarchy and Ghaddafi's revolutionary regime and quickly became the Polisario's largest supplier of arms. In October 1984, the ELPS unleashed its "Great Magreb Offensive" against the Berm under construction to the south of Saac, employing Soviet BMP-1s armed with Sagger antitank missiles. Thereafter, as the Moroccan strategic aim of enclosing most of Western Sahara became clear, the ELPS increased its offensive operations. As the Moroccans had planned, however, the Polisario forces now had to employ the kind of direct, costly, and concentrated attacks that they had previously sought to avoid. The Moroccans generally preferred to respond to Polisario attacks with firepower alone, declining to abandon the protection afforded by the defensive barriers. Indeed, on the occasions when they have done so, the Moroccans suffered heavy losses. Foreign military presence continued on both sides through the 1980s, including 500 Cuban and 25 North Korean technical advisors in Polisario training camps in Tinduf, and French and Israeli advisors with Moroccan military forces.[102]

Although restrictions on its freedom of movement grew and the Berm construction continued, the ELPS continued to display considerable tactical skills and remained capable of causing major problems for Morocco. A particularly bad year for the FAR was 1987, during which the FAR suffered at least 16 major attacks by Polisario forces. One of the most damaging, carried out in late-February near the border area near El Farsi, illustrates typical Polisario tactics against the Berm defenses. The immediate area was defended by only two small garrisons, manned by 80 and 50 Moroccan soldiers, respectively. The Polisario column approached the Berm under the cover of night, avoiding detection by the defenders. In the first phase, two mechanized battalions attacked, followed by an assault by a tank battalion. This method followed the general pattern of such operations: simultaneous attacks, one primary and one secondary, against two contiguous, mutually supporting defensive positions. The initial aim was to fix and hold the Moroccan defensive positions, thereby permitting mechanized and armored elements to break through to the other side of the Berm. There they awaited the arrival of the Moroccan rapid reaction force, which they ambushed with great effectiveness when it arrived. Another Polisario motorized battalion provided logistical support and transported captured materiel and prisoners to the rear. In this case, the magnitude of the FAR defeat was so great that Hassan II solicited a report from the general in charge of the southern provinces that evening. The report attributed the Moroccan debacle to a failure in intelligence, a lack of anti-tank weapons, and weaknesses in the armored intervention detachment.[103]

Even worse tactical defeats for the FAR ensued, revealing a recurring failure of commanders to foresee the locations of coming attacks. To make matters worse for the FAR, the soldiers in their garrisons frequently appeared to lack a strong fighting spirit. The Polisario learned that it could sometimes forgo frontal attacks; infiltrating through unguarded areas and then surrounding FAR positions might be all it took to make them surrender.[104] At the operational level, the Polisario launched attacks on different areas of the wall simultaneously, thereby diverting the rapid reaction forces.[105] Moreover, the Moroccan air forces sometimes failed to appear during major engagements with the ELPS. A fear of Polisario anti-air defenses, including the AA SAM 8 (GECKO) missiles, and poor ground-air coordination and communications technology probably explains this failing.[106] On the other hand, Moroccan combat engineers—"the unsung heroes of the war"—worked diligently, and often under fire, to construct and maintain the growing system of walls, which both sides realized were making a gradual but undeniable difference in the war's overall strategic outlook.[107]

The ELPS continued to undertake some major operations each year through 1989, and Morocco attacked Polisario positions in its section of Western Sahara in August 1991, breaking a ceasefire that had held since the onset of the previous year. But by this point, neither side saw a resolution through military force as a viable possibility.[108] Hence, when the UN Secretary General unilaterally declared a ceasefire in September, both sides chose to respect it, and the conflict has continued mainly in the diplomatic sphere. Many Sahrawis express negative opinions about MINURSO—tasked with monitoring the ceasefire and organizing and conducting a referendum—charging that it does little to stop abuses or break free of close Moroccan supervision and monitoring of its activities. Nonetheless, the ceasefire continues to hold.[109]

Military Occupation, Intifadas, and Arab Spring, 1991-2012.

After the ceasefire, Morocco and the Polisario both made intense use of diplomatic and international public relations endeavors, although, in general, Morocco made scant attempts to win Sahrawi hearts and minds.[110] The diplomatic and international legal aspects of the Western Sahara issue are not the primary focus of this monograph, but it is worth stressing that the failure to reach a solution did not result from a lack of outside interest in the problem, even if potential key players—especially Washington and Paris—might be faulted for not applying more pressure on Morocco. The UN, most visibly in the figure of envoy James Baker, exerted considerable efforts trying to resolve the conflict. In June 2001, the UN Secretary General's proposed framework agreement, known as the Baker Plan, called for elected executive and legislative bodies and much local control in Western Sahara, with a referendum on the status of the territory to be held within 5 years. After this proposal failed to gain sufficient support from the interested parties (Morocco, the Polisario, Mauritania, and Algeria), Baker proposed a compromise in January 2003, sometimes referred to as Baker Plan II, which was incorporated into the Secretary General's report of May 23, 2003. It did not require the consent of the four parties of Baker Plan I and gave voters in a future referendum the choice between integration with Morocco, autonomy, or independence. The Polisario, under pressure from Algeria, made the surprising announcement that it would support the proposal, but Morocco rejected it. In June 2004, Baker resigned, and the Baker Plan has not come up in Security Council Resolutions since.[111]

Morocco's objections stemmed principally from its rejection of the independence option; autonomy was as far as it would go. In addition, Rabat wanted to negotiate only with Algeria, but the latter insisted that it could not substitute for the Sahrawis. The issue of who should vote in any referendum has also been a major obstacle to successful negotiations, as the different parties interpret census figures and the role settlers should play differently, and neither side has wanted to risk a referendum it might lose. With Baker Plan II, however, the Polisario apparently thought independence was worth the risk, whereas Rabat may have feared that it had lost support among the Moroccan settlers, especially those of ethnic Sahrawi background who had moved to the territory in the 1990s. The Polisario's insistence on full independence and Morocco's refusal to consider this option have also remained a significant hindrance. Moreover, Rabat has felt less pressure to make concessions since the May 2003 Casablanca terrorist bombings, which further strengthened the post-9/11 strategic alliance between the United States and Morocco. In the fall of that year, President George W. Bush reportedly reassured King Mohammed VI that the United States would not seek to impose a solution on the Western Sahara impasse.[112]

As the diplomacy ran its course, the situation in the refugee camps in Algeria and the occupied and unoccupied territories of Western Sahara evolved into a distinct set of security challenges of relevance not only to the immediate players in the region, but also to the United States and other outside powers. According to the UN High Commissioner for Refugees (ACNUR), there are more than 116,000 Western Saharan refugees, and the camps in Algeria are home to 80,000 people. The situation of the refugees, while not as dire as in many of the world's camps for displaced people, remained a major concern even after the ceasefire. According to a 2008 study by ACNUR, the World Food Programme, and Médicos del Mundo, malnutrition affected 61 percent of children and 55 percent of women in the camps, contributing to high fetal death rates. There are also problems with the quality and quantity of water available in the camps, which are subject to disastrous flooding during periods of high rain.[113] The camps also lack adequate supplies of medicine. In fact, even after recent kidnappings, Spanish aid workers expressed a desire to remain and help alleviate the situation — warning that their absence would contribute to further economic hardship, in turn making the camps more vulnerable to radical movements.[114]

Nonetheless, the situation in the Polisario-run camps is far better than that in other refugee camps in Africa and elsewhere, generating "unknown levels of human development in the African context," writes an historian who, in other ways, is critical of the Polisario.[115] The Polisario's administration of the camps, which until the 1991 ceasefire was largely in the hands of women because the men were off to war, had many successes. Thanks to the extensive system of bilingual schools (Arabic and Spanish) and further education opportunities made available to Sahrawis over the years in Cuba and, to a lesser extent, in Algeria, Libya, Syria, the former Eastern Bloc countries, and even Spain, West Germany, and Austria, the educational level of the camps' residents is very high.

Indeed, underemployment is a major source of dissatisfaction for many of the Sahrawis educated abroad. In the field of health care, supplies may be short, but knowledge is not. The Tindouf camps have one doctor for every 800-1,000 residents, and in the unoccupied territory, Polisario-run clinics and military hospitals have also provided care to nomads from Mauritania, Algeria, and Mali.[116]

In addition to the UN and nongovernmental organizations (NGOs), several other sources of outside support help sustain life in the camps. Spain's Ministry of Defense pays pensions for Sahrawi veterans of the colonial period's *Tropas Nómadas* (Nomadic Troops) and *Policía Territorial* (Territorial Police Force), and Spaniards and other Europeans have donated much money to Sahrawi causes. Sahrawis who work abroad also send funds to family members in the camps. A major source of support for Western Saharans is the *Vacaciones en Paz* (Vacation in Peace) program, which sponsors 2-month summer visits each year by thousands of Western Saharan children between 8 and 12 years old to families in Spain and, to a lesser extent, Italy and France. The Spaniards in turn often visit these children and their families in the camps, bringing financial assistance when they come. Since 1991, a market economy has sprouted in the camps, which now host many small businesses such as Internet and telephone cafes (*locutorios*), hair salons, and small shops catering to residents and visitors alike, and enterprising Sahrawis have learned to profit by importing various goods from abroad. [117] In spite of this economic growth, however, some of the camps' younger residents have grown increasingly impatient with the situation, some openly expressing a desire to go to war again.[118]

Morocco has strongly criticized the Polisario's leadership and management of the camps, sometimes describing them as a virtual reign of terror and making good use of the criticism by defectors from the Polisario. Even researchers sympathetic to the Polisario note that treatment of dissidents has been harsh, especially during the high point of the war with Morocco. These researchers write of purges of those considered dangerous to the "revolution" and of Sahrawis who promote "tribalism."[119] Human Rights Watch and representatives of the UN and NGOs, on the other hand, have been much less critical, especially of the situation since the ceasefire. According to a 2008 Human Rights Watch report, "The Polisario effectively marginalizes those who directly challenge its leadership or general political orientation, but it does not imprison them. It allows residents to criticize its day-to-day administration of camp affairs." If they wish to do so, residents of the camps in Algeria may also move to Moroccan-controlled Western Saharan territory through Mauritania, although "fear and social pressure" keeps them from disclosing their plans in advance.[120] Some Spanish NGO workers have even praised the Polisario for providing security against possible extremist infiltration and terrorist threats.[121] The principal Sahrawi security forces are the Sahrawi National Police, which operate in the camps, and the National Gendarmerie, whose jurisdiction includes the roads and trails between the camps, nearby Polisario institutions, and the part of Western Sahara not occupied by Morocco. The Gendarmerie, with its more military structure and jurisdiction over transportation routes, is tasked with countering smuggling and — one would assume — more recent threats of penetration by terrorists and criminal organizations.[122]

In the camps and elsewhere, the social situation of Sahrawis today has some peculiar aspects. Cuba has sponsored study by thousands of young Sahrawis in secondary schools, universities, technical institutes, and military academies. Upon their return to Western Sahara, many experienced a sort of reverse culture shock, wondering how to put their education to use in the desert and feeling constrained by many aspects of traditional Sahrawi society. Saharan women who had studied in Cuba, for example, found themselves stereotyped as promiscuous, and people began to joke that the male and female *cubarauis* as a whole constituted a new Saharan tribe with its own identity. Returnees from Cuba figure prominently among the new generation of Sahrawi elite, who question the dominance and ways of the traditional Polisario leadership without renouncing its cause.[123]

Since the ceasefire, the Polisario has continued to receive criticism for corruption, authoritarianism, and repression of dissent.[124] Not surprisingly, many of these negative reports come from the growing list of former Polisario officials—some of whom previously held very high positions in the organization—who have defected to the Moroccan side since 1975. As one would expect, in the sphere of public relations, Morocco has done its best to extract the maximum possible gain from these cases. On more than a few occasions, the principal motives of these people, dismissed as opportunistic traitors by the Polisario, were undoubtedly financial; Morocco offered attractive incentives to those Sahrawis who publicly denounced the Polisario. In other cases, however, the situation was not so clear-cut. Some Sahrawis seem to have concluded, albeit reluctantly, that the Polisario's strategic goal of full independence was no longer realistic, seeing some sort of autonomy statute as the best they could hope for. Others claim that they became turned off by the Polisario's intransigence and unwillingness to consider opposing views.[125] Some may also see hope in King Mohammed VI's initiatives, however halting and incomplete, to begin to address the issue of the disappearances and to institute a committee of reconciliation, although there is still good reason to view these gestures with some cynicism, as is also the case with his Arab Spring-inspired reforms.

Mohammed VI established the reconciliation committee in 2004 to shed light on the issue of forced disappearances and arbitrary detentions from the period of 1956, when Morocco gained independence, through 1999. After 2 years of work, the committee issued a report with its findings on 742 disappearances, the majority of which were related to the Sahara. According to the report, all had ended in death — either in captivity, in clashes with Moroccan forces, or because of excessively violent actions against demonstrations. But as Amnesty International reports, the government has not published the list of names, and some 500 cases involving Sahrawis remain in process.[126]

From 1975 on, the anti-nationalist repression of the Sahrawis by Moroccan authorities was severe, and estimates of the total number of "disappeared" in the Western Sahara since the Spanish withdrawal range from several hundred to over 1,000. The last great wave of disappearances occurred in November 1987, coinciding roughly with a visit by a UN technical mission. These large-scale detentions by Moroccan authorities acquired a permanent character; many lasted until June 1991, when over 300 of the "disappeared" Sahrawis were released. The former detainees have spoken of clandestine prisons, harsh conditions, and physical and psychological abuse while in Moroccan custody.[127] As of June 2010, there were reportedly 46 Sahrawi political prisoners in various facilities in Morocco and in the so-called "black prison" of El Aaiún.[128]

For its part, the Polisario took over 2000 Moroccan prisoners of war beginning in 1976. With the mediation of U.S. Senator Richard Lugar and the International Red Cross, the last 404 Moroccan prisoners were released in 2005. Many had been held captive by the Polisario since the late-1980s, and they subsequently spoke of harsh conditions, abuse, forced labor, and being paraded before visiting journalists and Spanish tourists by the Polisario. In many cases, Morocco refused to accept the former prisoners upon their release because Rabat would not recognize the Polisario. The return of these prisoners was thus delayed by years, until diplomats from the United States and Argentina forcibly repatriated them.[129]

The human rights record of Morocco in general is not a good one, even outside of Western Sahara. Although the record does not look so bad compared with that of other regimes in North Africa and the Middle East, it is not a country of ample political freedom — improvements since the coronation of Mohammed VI in 1999, notwithstanding. As Human Rights Watch and Amnesty International have noted, the regime has traditionally shown no toleration for opposing views in three areas: the monarchy, Islam, and the territorial integrity of the kingdom. The latter, of course, pertains directly to the Western Sahara question. A Freedom House report from 2009 categorized Western Sahara to be one of the 21 most repressive societies in the world. In a 2010 report, Human Rights Watch noted that the Moroccan government's methods were especially harsh in Western Sahara, where Sahrawis were arrested or imprisoned for peaceful defense of self-determination, while politically motivated travel restrictions increased.[130] The U.S. State Department's April 2011 report on human rights refers to "arbitrary and unlawful killings" by Moroccan government security officials, "unconfirmed reports of politically motivated disappearance," and "credible reports that security forces engage in torture, beatings, and other mistreatment of detainees," especially Sahrawi separatist activists.[131]

On the other hand, since the 1990s, the monarchy has embarked on a process of gradual but undeniable political democratization, although the country still has a long way to go. Concurrently, freedom of expression about the monarchy and other subjects in Morocco increased during this period, although periodicals that offended the monarchy were eventually shut down, some only reemerging very recently as online publications.[132] The king's response to the Arab Spring, revealing an apparent willingness to consider such formerly off-limits topics as the sacred status of the monarchy, indicates that further opening is occurring, although it remains to be seen exactly what tangible changes the new constitution of July 2011 will bring. Critics charge that the constitution calls for scant meaningful reforms, leaving the king's privileges and the traditional system of patronage and clientelism largely untouched.[133]

In the economic sphere, the Moroccan government has undeniably made considerable investments in the Western Saharan territory it controls. Although it has had to spend enormous amounts of money in military and security costs and infrastructure, the regime has reaped at least some economic gain for its efforts. For example, fishing is among the most profitable Western Saharan natural resources, as evidenced by the sardine canning facilities at El Aaiún, which employ more than 1,000 people. Waters off the Western Saharan coast generate more than 60 percent of Morocco's fishing activities and revenues, creating more than 50,000 jobs. Yet, many Sahrawis complain that they have gained little from these investments, which they say primarily benefit the Moroccan settlers and people with good political connections. Ties between the fishing industry, high military figures, and people near to the throne are close.[134] In other spheres of commercial activity there is a strong perception that Sahrawis — with the exception of the high-level "defectors" — are not benefiting from the economic development taking place. For example, Imazighen (Berbers) from the Sus and the Anti-Atlas, who often work as merchants, operate many of the cafes, shops, and hotels in the Western Sahara. But they keep their permanent homes elsewhere, where they often send their income. Unemployment is officially 25 percent in the region, but it may, in fact, be twice that.[135]

This situation illustrates a more general problem, which exacerbated the consequences of Morocco's lack of attempts to win hearts and minds in Western Sahara, even as the main force of Sahrawi nationalism shifted from the refugee camps to the occupied territories during the 1990s.[136] Cronyism, a spoils system, and misgovernance do little to foment an entrepreneurial spirit or genuine belief in the legitimacy of the Moroccan state, rewarding only good connections and political loyalty. In fact, the roots of recent violent confrontations at El Aaiún in November 2010, disturbing footage of which has been disseminated on *YouTube*, lay in popular anger over the embezzlement of land designated for indigenous Sahrawis.[137] The riots, described in one account as "the most violent 48 hours witnessed by the Western Sahara" since the 1991 ceasefire began, predictably led to accusations, counteraccusations, and attempts by both sides to package favorably images of the bloody fighting for the international media and the Internet.[138] Moroccan authorities reportedly brought into custody about 200 Sahrawis after the riots, many of whom then faced trial in a military court near Rabat. On the other hand, the nomination of a new *wali* of the region within weeks of the riots indicates that the monarchy had taken the causes of the protests seriously.[139]

Of course, such complaints about favoritism, corruption, and anti-Sahrawi discrimination are not new. During the late-Spanish period, they fueled youthful resentment against colonial authorities and their collaborators, and thereafter they contributed to what are known as the intifadas of 1999 and 2005. Other causes of these generally nonviolent popular protests were cultural, such as the belief that Morocco aims to eradicate Sahrawi culture, linguistic and otherwise. It does not help that soldiers make up about one-third of the Moroccan population of Western Sahara, not counting the various kinds of police, state security, and intelligence personnel.[140] In addition to socio-cultural and economic complaints, disappointments on the political and diplomatic stage also contributed to the intifadas.

The intifada of late-1999 took place at least in part for the benefit of the international community, occurring as it did after the death of Hassan II, when the initial weeks after the takeover by his son, Mohammed, seemed to promise democratic reform. The 2005 intifada occurred in the wake of the growing realization by Sahrawis that Polisario diplomacy had not managed to persuade the heavy-hitting outside powers (especially the United States) to withdraw their customary support for the Moroccan position; receiving little help from Washington for his efforts, Baker had resigned in June 2004. Significantly, the popular demonstrations apparently occurred, at least in part, outside the control of the Polisario leadership, suggesting that young people were rejecting the approach of some of the traditional Sahrawi elites. Many leading organizers of the demonstrations, however, had reportedly spent long periods in Moroccan prisons.[141]

Morocco's harsh response to the 1999 and 2005 intifadas may have exacerbated the situation. The first intifada, which began with dozens of students organizing a sit-in, setting up tents, and occupying a square in front of a hotel where many UN personnel stayed, provoked a Moroccan reaction of "excessive violence," in the words of a U.S. State Department employee.[142] But thereafter, Morocco removed the governor and local chief of police, announced elections for a Saharan affairs council, and freed some political prisoners. The government's direction reversed itself, however, after the terrorist bombings in Casablanca on May 16, 2003, when it again clamped down on some Sahrawi activists, along with the Islamists who made up the primary targets of the crackdown. A low point in the Moroccan response to the second intifada occurred in October 2005, when security forces publicly beat a Sahrawi demonstrator to death, making him the intifada's first martyr. Predictably, his funeral in January 2006 was a massive, although silent, demonstration. When the activist Aminatou Haidar was then released from prison, crowds responded with open demonstrations of support for SADR, with some demonstrators sporting Palestinian-style headscarves in apparent attempts of provocation.[143]

Several points about the intifadas merit special mention. First, some ethnic Sahrawis living in parts of Morocco and poor Moroccans in Western Sahara joined the demonstrations against the Moroccan authorities and the status quo.[144] Although the two groups by no means constitute a united front, the settlers in Western Sahara, along with the Moroccans of Sahrawi ethnicity in nearby areas such as Tarfaya, are not necessarily unequivocal supporters of the Moroccan regime and the status quo. Indeed, some of the settlers may have become so dissatisfied with Rabat with time that they came to favor the Polisario's position.[145]

Second, the role of technology, especially in the second intifada, was striking. The Internet and mobile phones have radically changed the playing field. Given the forced separation of so many families and friends between the refugee camps and on both sides of the Berm, it is hardly surprising that Sahrawis learned to make good use of the Internet. In ways that foreshadowed the Arab Spring, the Internet and mobile phones enabled the coordination of demonstrations and the recording of images for political purposes, and their role in protests in 2010 and thereafter shows that their importance has only increased in the meantime.[146] Indeed, some activists have traced the origins of the Arab Spring to Western Sahara.[147]

Since the second intifada, another set of security concerns in Western Sahara has arisen. Worrisome elements from the Sahel have shown some signs of attempting to infiltrate the refugee camps and Western Sahara. These include the drug trade (with links to South America) and Islamist terrorist organizations. In 2010, Mali arrested six major drug traffickers linked to a criminal gang with ties to al-Qaeda in the Islamic Maghreb (AQIM), and the Malians identified the arrestees as "coming from the ranks of the Polisario Front."[148] More recently, in October 2011, an armed group kidnapped three European aid workers from Sahrawi refugee camps outside of Tindouf, Algeria. An AQIM splinter faction eventually claimed responsibility, although the circumstances and authors of the kidnappings remain unclear.[149] This event came after the kidnapping of three Spaniards in November 2009 in northwest Mauritania, for which AQIM claimed responsibility. This abduction reportedly resulted in the payment of an enormous ransom by Madrid and the freeing of Omar Sid'Ahmed Ould Hamma, also known as Omar the Sahrawi, who was reportedly a former member of the Polisario hierarchy. Morocco has drawn as much attention as possible to these alleged connections between the Polisario and terrorism. The few known instances of cooperation between Sahrawis and AQIM apparently stemmed from financial rather than ideological motives.[150] But such unnatural alliances can constitute real threats nonetheless, and AQIM has shown a willingness to seek help from those not necessarily sharing its worldview, such as criminal elements active in kidnapping and the drug trade. The alleged mercenary work by some Sahrawis for Libyan dictator Muammar Gaddafi during his last days, to which Morocco was quick to draw attention, probably stemmed mostly from financial motives.

Nevertheless, given the conditions in the massive camps and the younger generation's lack of hope for a better future, it would be most surprising if radical Islamist ideology found no converts whatsoever. Some Sahrawis have expressed the belief that, were Islamists to overthrow Mohammed VI, the new regime in Rabat would pull Morocco out of Western Sahara.[151] This apparently naive view may not have many adherents, but if widely believed, it could give the Sahrawis a reason to support the religious extremists, although this possibility seems remote. In any case, terrorist organizations will undoubtedly try to gain a foothold in the Western Sahara if at all possible, as they now do in northern Mali. There, three organizations, AQIM, the Movement for Unity and Jihad in West Africa, and Ansar al Din, have combined forces since January 2012 to attempt to impose an ultra-strict observance of Islamic law that runs counter to the region's traditionally more tolerant and open practices.[152]

RECOMMENDATIONS

When evaluating the current situation in Western Sahara and making decisions about any role the United States could or should play in the conflict, military planners and policymakers would do well to keep several considerations in mind.

1. At the most basic level, the U.S. Army should make better use of the military history of Western Sahara as a source of relevant and concrete knowledge, in particular with regard to the role of fortified walls (the Berm) in COIN, static defense strategy in general, and guerrilla tactics of possible relevance to future irregular operations. As we have seen, modern U.S.-trained and supplied military forces such as the FAR can suffer significant tactical and even operational-level setbacks at the hands of able enemies like the Polisario. In an age of rapid dissemination of news from the battlefront, tactical successes such as those inflicted by the Polisario against the Berm can have strategic and grand strategic significance, especially

in the theater of public opinion. Moreover, in a future conflict in the area with more direct involvement by the United States and more extensive media coverage, the overall impact of tactical developments would be deeper. Even the authoritarian regime in Rabat, which has more control over the dissemination of news than a democratic government does, had to overcome political difficulties stemming from tactical defeats at the hands of the Polisario.

The tactical and operational aspects of the Polisario war and their relationship to strategy, covered previously, still need further study by military historians and analysts. Although the Berm-based strategy of static defense enabled Morocco to gain control of much of Western Sahara, it did not bring with it a decisive defeat of the enemy. Given the likelihood that any future U.S. military intervention in this area, as in the Sahel, would most likely involve special forces or other nonconventional units, the knowledge of Polisario tactics and ways of wars in general could also prove useful, as could a better understanding of Morocco and Mauritania's experiences in combatting them. In addition, learning more about the military history of the conflict could help military planners gain a better idea of what to expect in future desert conflicts, especially of this type in this region. The Western Sahara experience reminds us that desert geography can still facilitate successful guerrilla operations, and the U.S. Army should make sure it has up-to-date and complete knowledge of the physical and human geography of the area at its disposal.

2. The U.S. Army should learn more about the Moroccan military and prepare for the possibility of more joint operations with it, drawing from the historical

lessons mentioned previously and an in-depth study of the FAR today. Given Morocco's importance for current AFRICOM issues, including terrorist threats from the Sahel and other potential sources of political instability, it makes sense to focus more on military forces with which the United States may soon cooperate more closely. As we have seen, limitations imposed from the top have historically hindered operational effectiveness, mission command on the ground, and air-land cooperation and coordination in the Moroccan military. In some cases, there may be some hesitation from above to give commanders too much leeway with U.S.-supplied new technologies, and training methods and goals will, of course, need to be adapted to the Moroccan military culture. In the unlikely event that war were to break out again involving the Western Sahara, Morocco, and Algeria, U.S. military planners will need to take into account the skills and limitations of the Moroccan armed forces and adjust their expectations accordingly. As this monograph has attempted to demonstrate, the history of the region also makes clear the importance of cultural knowledge and effective civil affairs work, intelligence analysis, geographical constraints, and familiarity with classical guerrilla methods in Western Sahara—with its specific set of human and physical geographical circumstances.

3. At the policy level, the strategic importance of Morocco to the United States, long a fundamental tenet of U.S. diplomacy in the region, is likely to increase even further, especially given the country's proximity to the Sahel and ongoing developments stemming from the Arab Spring. Yet, the Western Sahara problem and related Moroccan affairs, however vital to the legitimacy and stability of the U.S. strategic partner-

ship with Rabat, often correspond more directly and immediately to Europe than to the United States for political, historical, and geographical reasons. In the economic sphere, natural resources in the region such as hydrocarbons and phosphate may prove important to the United States over the long term, but at present, gas supplies and security-related issues of terrorism, the drug trade, and immigration are of more direct concern to Europe.

Hence, Europe should lead mediation efforts. Moreover, some powers, such as France, are likely to react badly if the United States acts unilaterally to exert pressure on Morocco. Cooperation with the French is, moreover, an important part of AFRICOM's activities today.

Yet, the United States still has a crucial, if somewhat less visible, role to play in resolving the Western Sahara problem. Above all, Washington should consider ways in which to leverage European powers, especially France and Spain, to take more decisive actions to solve current problems in the region. U.S. military and economic policies and support could be tied to concrete efforts by Europe to promote a settlement that, in theory, could bring benefits to all the interested parties. If left alone, the situation will probably deteriorate, and a regime change in Morocco might well signify strategic disaster for the United States. Hence, while it may be most appropriate for European countries to implement directly some of the recommendations that follow, the United States should explore ways to encourage the relevant governments to act accordingly.

4. The United States should continue to monitor closely the security situation in Western Sahara and its possible relationship to developments in the Sahel, co-

operating with Moroccan intelligence collection agencies but working to curtail their repressive practices. As we have seen, the failure by military leaders to grasp changing socio-political conditions contributed decisively to the decline of colonial authority in the decade or so before Spain's withdrawal. Today, once again, the younger generation of Sahrawis is growing increasingly dissatisfied with the current situation. Pernicious influences from the Sahel, including the drug trade, kidnapping, and AQIM, have the potential to constitute a threat in the massive refugee camps and among the increasingly restive youth of both the Moroccan-controlled and the unoccupied territories.[153] Furthermore, effective action against terrorist and criminal activity in North Africa entails regional cooperation, but Western Sahara remains a source of conflict between Morocco and Algeria. Indeed, one of the last major closed borders in the world continues to separate these two countries.

As the younger generation of Sahrawis loses its patience, some of its members may eventually embrace more radical outlooks. Others may be willing to sell their geographical familiarity and navigational skills in the region to terrorists, drug traffickers, or other criminal elements for the right price. Regardless of a lack of ideological affinities, some Sahrawis have apparently demonstrated a willingness to cooperate with groups working actively against the United States and its allies. As long as dissatisfaction with the current situation in Western Sahara and the refugee camps persists, the potential for cooperation with anti-American elements will remain. Economic problems affecting Spain and other traditional sources of humanitarian and financial aid, along with rising security threats, may well increase hardships in the camps and unoccupied territories. Adding to the potential sources of future unrest, food prices are expected to rise worldwide.

In spite of the undeniable possibility of terrorist connections and other security threats in the region, however, it is far from inevitable that Western Sahara or the camps will fall to Islamist terrorism. With its rational political goals and methods, the Polisario leadership has long tried to avoid alienating Western powers, and it shares little, if any, of the worldview of Islamic extremists. The "Islamist wave" that has entered Morocco over the last 2 decades largely missed Western Sahara, although the movement does have numerous adherents among the many Moroccan military personnel stationed in the territory.[154] There seems to have been scant Sahrawi presence among the thousands of North Africans who joined the struggle of Afghan mujahedin against the Soviet Union, spent time in radical Islamist training camps in Afghanistan or Pakistan, or joined more recent Jihadist endeavors in Iraq.

One should thus be wary of claims that the traditional political aims of the Polisario are being overtaken by an Islamist wave of future terrorists. Deeply rooted, relatively modern attitudes promoted by a Polisario leadership that prizes Western support are not going to disappear overnight. Moreover, the Polisario has apparently increased its security and keeps up its guard against terrorist infiltration enough to inspire the confidence of foreign humanitarian workers, who express a strong desire to remain even after the well-publicized kidnappings. Indeed, these workers reason that one of the best ways to keep terrorists out is to fight economic and medical hardships in the camps.[155]

Admittedly, NGO officials sometimes display a naivety about dangers from within the communities they are trying to help. By the same token, however, defense and security analysts can be prone to generalizing and exaggerating threats, inadvertently leaving possible collaborators from within target communities overlooked. Of course, Morocco's emphasis on the vulnerability of the Polisario-controlled camps to penetration by terrorist and criminal groups, however self-serving, has some plausibility, and an independent Western Sahara might well have a hard time keeping down serious security threats. On the other hand, the Polisario claims that it combats terrorism better than the Moroccan government.[156] Hence, while the possibility of Islamist terrorist groups taking root in Western Sahara exists, there are plenty of elements working against the fruition of such a movement there, and the United States could conceivably use these elements to its advantage. Indeed, in the admittedly unlikely scenario that an extremist Islamist regime were to take over in Rabat, Western Sahara might actually serve as one of the few areas in the region where Europeans and Americans could maintain a foothold.

The Cuban-educated Sahrawis, the so-called *cubarauis,* make up a good portion of Western Sahara's non-Moroccan elite and are probably least susceptible to Islamist influences. Although it may seem counterintuitive for the United States to reach out to the products of Marxist education and training, the modern-thinking *cubarauis* should not be dismissed as possible allies in attempts to keep terrorist movements from infiltrating Western Saharan society. Indeed, the Cuban connection may have helped make Sahrawi society less amenable to overtures from organizations and ideologies of the al-Qaeda variety, helping maintain the region as a partial bulwark against Islamist extremism. Combined with the Polisario's paradoxical roots in revolutionary Algerian ideology, Soviet influence, modern Islam, and its often pro-Western diplomatic slant, the *cubarauis* have helped give Western Sahara a relatively modern outlook. Democratization can, of course, lead to a rise in political parties of strong religious orientations, as we have seen in Egypt, Tunisia, and elsewhere, and this possibility cannot be dismissed outright. Nonetheless, such a development appears less likely in Western Sahara.

5. There is a strong strategic interest in supporting a program of autonomy for Western Sahara, as the United States has already affirmed. But efforts must be made to ensure that the autonomy is genuine and accompanied by tangible improvements in human rights and democratization. At this point, full independence, however justifiable from the perspective of international law, history, or moral grounds, is not a realistic solution. At the most basic level, it would weaken the monarchy considerably were Mohammed VI to "lose" Western Sahara, upon which the Alawi dynasty has long—and with no small amount of success—based its legitimacy. If Islamist extremists were to topple the monarchy, the ramifications for the region and for Europe would be severe. The concerns of Algeria, which supplies much of southern Europe's natural gas, should be taken into account as well. Ideally, it should be possible to craft a solution that offers gains to Morocco, Algeria, and the Polisario.

In the area of human rights, the creation of some sort of supervisory mechanism, probably through MINURSO, would fill a major gap in the effectiveness of the current UN presence. It would also demonstrate that the international community takes the concerns of the Sahrawis seriously, possibly limiting the appeal of extremists promising more radical solutions. As a Spanish policy think tank argued in 2011, cooperation between London and Madrid could help overcome any French resistance to this idea. [157] The United States should consider supporting this proposal as well.

Thus, without going so far as to threaten the stability of the Alawi monarchy, the United States and Europe should strongly encourage Morocco to develop and implement a program of genuine autonomy for Western Sahara. Ensuring France's cooperation in these endeavors should be a priority. Sahrawi skepticism about Rabat's intentions is well grounded; only through genuine reforms, autonomy, and a significant reduction in clientelism and corruption does the Moroccan government stand a chance of gaining some credibility among the Sahrawis. By putting more pressure on Morocco, moreover, the United States may gain credibility among the Polisario and Algeria, whose support could be crucial for a lasting settlement.

Admittedly, significant barriers to the successful implementation of true autonomy remain. Spain's constitutional structure of autonomous regions, sometimes cited as a possible model for Morocco's future, helped make possible a remarkably peaceful transition from dictatorship to democracy after the death of General Francisco Franco in 1975. But a West European democracy such as Spain differs considerably from Morocco's authoritarian state. In Spain, moreover, the regions with the strongest independence movements, Catalonia and the Basque Country, also have very healthy and modernized economies, which is definitely not the case for Western Sahara. As noted previously, autonomy statutes in nondemocratic states have a bad track record.

In Morocco, the high levels of corruption and the opaqueness of governmental processes and appointments cast serious doubt on whether Sahrawis will believe they can get a fair shake in any promised autonomy arrangement. Indeed, developments up to this point indicate the opposite. The Spanish policy of buying off elites, discussed previously, failed over the long term, and there are signs that the Moroccan practice of allowing the high-level defectors from the Polisario to profit immensely while the financial status of the majority remains very low may backfire as well. Further, periods of transition and regime change are notoriously dangerous for minorities, as the experiences of post-colonial Middle Eastern Jews, Christians in Iraq today, and many other cases illustrate. Along these lines, among those in the political opposition in Morocco, signs of resentment of the Sahrawis and of economic development in Western Sahara have surfaced recently.[158]

On the other hand, the promotion of genuine autonomy for Western Sahara would go well with the current U.S. position of supporting Arab Spring-era democratization in Libya, Egypt, and elsewhere. Since before the Arab Spring, the Moroccan monarchy has taken some clear steps in the direction of constitutional reform and democracy, but it still has a long way to go, and critics rightly charge that many of the changes appear more cosmetic than real. A decisive step toward democracy in Morocco might help the regime avoid the most radical manifestations of the Arab Spring and help convince the Sahrawis that the crown's promises of autonomy are genuine.

At the same time, Sahrawi nationalist leaders are much more likely to support an autonomy proposal coming from Rabat if they believe the United States and Western Europe (especially France) will compel Morocco to keep its promises. Along these lines, it would serve U.S. interests for Washington, Paris, and others to pressure Morocco to address human rights issues in Western Sahara and elsewhere more fully. A failure to do so will cause the United States to lose credibility among Sahrawis — the older generation of which long revealed a remarkable faith in the efficacy of its diplomatic efforts to win Western sympathies. As we have seen, however, this faith has dissipated at least somewhat.

6. The United States political and military leaders should continue to draw upon the military, diplomatic, and economic ties of Spain and France to the region, which are also grounded in history and geography. These ties complement the mission of AFRICOM and its support of the Trans Sahara Counter Terrorism Partnership (TSCTP) program, the members of which are Morocco, Algeria, Tunisia, Chad, Mali, Mauritania, Niger, Nigeria, Senegal, and the United States.[159] Although no European countries are now members of the partnership, existing programs of cooperation between European and African militaries may bring operational advantages.

Moreover, even in the current climate of economic crisis, European countries are increasing their military involvement in the Sahel. Spain and France, for instance, have made it clear that they consider developments in the Sahel to be a significant threat. The Spanish general staff has begun studying closer cooperation with France and the United States in the Sahel area, which it perceives as a source of future troubles in Western Sahara.[160] Recent kidnappings underscore the growing awareness in Spain of a need for further involvement in the region. Although the financially strapped Spanish military currently lacks materiel resources, it can offer relevant experience and intelligence. France has similar experience and intelligence in the region, and it also has more influence in Rabat today. Tellingly, after the fall of Tunisian and Egyptian leaders, Mohammed VI and leading Moroccan security and military advisors traveled to France in late-January 2011 for meetings with the French government.[161] The French, moreover, will most likely make the largest contribution to a coming operation in Mali, which is a response to recent terrorist activities in the Sahel.[162] Paris will probably not react well if Washington takes any unilateral actions in the region, and the United States currently depends heavily on French experience and intelligence in the Sahel.

Finally, the Polisario should have a place in any relevant negotiations, and the Western Sahara issue as a whole must be taken into account in any policy decisions pertaining to Morocco, Algeria, Mauritania, or even developments in the Sahel in general. In theory, at least, an agreement with something to offer all of the parties is not beyond reach. A failure to find an adequate solution to Western Sahara could lead to a further destabilizing of the region and of a key U.S. ally, Morocco.

ENDNOTES

1. Jacob Mundy, "The Morocco-Polisario War for Western Sahara, 1975-1991," in Barry Rubin, ed., *Conflict and Insurgency in the Contemporary Middle East*, New York: Routledge, 2009, p. 224.

2. George McGovern, "Foreword," in Stephen Zunes and Jacob Mundy, *Western Sahara: War, Nationalism, and Conflict Irresolution*, Syracuse, NY: Syracuse University Press, 2010, p. xiv.

3. Cited in Zunes and Mundy, p. 162; Eduardo Soto-Trillo, *Viaje al abandono. Por qué no permiten al Sáhara ser libre (Journey to Abandonment: Why the Sahara Is Not Allowed to be Free)*, Madrid, Spain: Santillana, 2011, p. 95.

4. Anouar Boukhars and Ali O. Amar, "Trouble in the Western Sahara," *The Journal of Middle East and Africa*, Vol. 2, No. 2, 2011, p. 232.

5. Zunes and Mundy, p. 160; Pablo San Martín, *Western Sahara: The Refugee Nation*. Cardiff, UK: University of Wales Press, 2010, p. 10.

6. Zunes and Mundy, p. 99.

7. Mariano Fernández-Aceytuno, *Ifni y Sáhara. Una encrucijada en la historia de España (Ifni and the Sahara: A Crossroads in the History of Spain)*, Dueñas, Spain: Simancas, 2001, pp. 418-424, 439-441; San Martín, *Western Sahara*, p. 69.

8. Fernández-Aceytuno, pp. 438, 551.

9. *Ibid.*, pp. 561-608.

10. José Ramón Diego Aguirre, *Guerra en el Sáhara*, Madrid, Spain: Istmo, 1991, pp. 49-50, 54, 67-68; Fernández-Aceytuno, pp. 189-190, 654-655; Soto-Trillo, pp. 251-254.

11. Diego Aguirre, p. 55.

12. Carlos Ruiz Miguel, *El Sáhara Occidental y España: historia, política y derecho. Análisis crítico de la política exterior española*

(*The Western Sahara and Spain: History, Politics, and Law: A Critical Analysis of Spanish Foreign Policy*), Madrid, Spain: Dykinson, 1995, p. 61. San Martín, *Western Sahara*, pp. 68, 71.

13. Fernández-Aceytuno, p. 424; Geoffrey Jensen, "The Peculiarities of 'Spanish Morocco': Imperial Ideology and Economic Development," *Mediterranean Historical Review*, Vol. 20, No. 1, 2005, pp. 80-101.

14. Fernández-Aceytuno, pp. 441, 621.

15. *Ibid.*, pp. 669-670.

16. Tomás Bárbulo, *La historia prohibida del Sáhara Español* (*The Forbidden History of the Spanish Sahara*), Barcelona, Spain: Destino, 2002, p. 41.

17. Ruiz Miguel, pp. 74-75; Fernández-Aceytuno, pp. 138, 669.

18. Zunes and Mundy, p. 95.

19. Anna Khakee, "The Western Saharan autonomy proposal and political reform in Morocco," *NOREF Report*, June 2011, pp. 1-12, available from *www.peacebuilding.no/var/ezflow_site/storage/original/application/a3acc871f1198e8e21bfc68ae75f8f48.pdf*.

20. Fernández-Aceytuno, pp. 652-654, 563; Diego Aguirre, p. 43.

21. Diego Aguirre, p. 63.

22. *Ibid.*, pp. 50-54; Fernández-Aceytuno, pp. 667ff.; Ignacio Fuente Cobo and Fernando M. Mariño Menéndez, *El conflicto del Sáhara occidental* (*The Western Sahara Conflict*), Madrid, Spain: Ministerio de Defensa, 2006, p. 30.

23. Fernández-Aceytuno, p. 671.

24. Zunes and Mundy, pp. 60-64; Diego Aguirre, pp. 112-118.

25. Bárbulo, pp. 266-282.

26. *Ibid.*, pp. 266-286; Fuente Cobo and Mariño Menéndez, p. 67.

27. Fuente Cobo and Mariño Menéndez, p. 68.

28. *Ibid.*, pp. 77-78, 112; Mundy, "The Morocco-Polisario War," pp. 215, 223.

29. Zunes and Mundy, pp. 8-22, 64-68; Belkace Hacene-Djaballah, "Conflict in Western Sahara: A Study of POLISARIO as an Insurgency Movement," Ph.D. dissertation, Catholic University of America, Washington DC, 1985, pp. 45-46.

30. Hacene-Djaballah, pp. 45-46; Zunes and Mundy, p. 22.

31. Fuente Cobo and Mariño Menéndez, p. 27.

32. Zunes and Mundy, p. 35.

33. Yolanda Sobero, *Sáhara. Memoria y olvido* (*The Sahara. Memory and Oblivion*), Barcelona, Spain: Ariel, 2010, p. 205; Soto-Trillo, p. 205.

34. Zunes and Mundy, p. 35; Chris Rhodes, "The Achilles Heel of Algal Biofuels: Peak Phosphate," *Forbes*, February 29, 2012, available from *www.forbes.com/sites/energysource/2012/02/29/the-achilles-heel-of-algal-biofuels-peak-phosphate-3/*.

35. Charles A. Rarick, Gideon Falk, and Casimir C. Barczyk, "An Element of Concern in North Africa: The Case of Morocco's Phosphate Industry," Purdue University Calumet, January 2, 2011, available from *papers.ssrn.com/sol3/Delivery.cfm?abstractid=1734142*.

36. Zunes and Mundy, p. xxii.

37. Sobero, pp. 213-214.

38. Soto-Trillo, pp. 233-234.

39. Zunes and Mundy, p. 228; ""Last oil company withdraws from Western Sahara," *Afrol News*, May 2, 2006, available from *www.afrol.com/articles/19029*.

40. Sobero, p. 213.

41. Zunes and Mundy, p. xxi; Human Rights Watch, *Human Rights in the Western Sahara and in the Tindouf Refugee Camps*, December 19, 2008, p. 8.

42. For example, Ángela Hernández Moreno, *Guerra de banderas en el Sáhara*, (*War of Flags in the Sahara*), Madrid, Spain: Entimema, 2006. Not surprisingly, this book has been translated into Arabic and published in Morocco. For a summary of the issue, see Zunes and Mundy, pp. 91-95.

43. Zunes and Mundy, pp. 94-98; Sobero, pp. 87-88, 247-250. See also San Martín, *Western Sahara*, pp. 35-40, and Diego Aguirre, pp. 28-38.

44. Fernández-Aceytuno, pp. 79-80, 653-654.

45. Zunes and Mundy, p. 58; Pablo San Martín, "´¡Estos locos cubarauis!´: The Hispanisation of Sahrawi society (…after Spain)," *Journal of Transatlantic Studies*, Vol 7, No. 3, September 2009, pp. 249-263; Soto-Trillo, p. 150.

46. Fernández-Aceytuno, pp. 68-70.

47. Soto-Trillo, p. 237.

48. Zunes and Mundy, p. 93.

49. Soto-Trillo, pp. 270, 280.

50. Fernández-Aceytuno, pp. 652-653; Diego Aguirre, pp. 41-47; Sobero, p. 88; Hacene-Djaballah, pp. 49, 79.

51. Fernández-Aceytuno, p. 654.

52. Ruiz Miguel, pp. 54-55; Zunes and Mundy, pp. 35-40.

53. Hacene-Djaballah, p. 43.

54. Quoted in San Martín, *Western Sahara*, p. 101.

55. Fuente Cobo and Meriño Menéndez, p. 71; Sobero, pp. 62-63.

56. Hernández-Moreno, p. 111; Hacene-Djaballah, p. 202.

57. Fuente Cobo and Meriño Menéndez, pp. 36-37.

58. Zunes and Mundy, p. 6.

59. Fernández-Aceytuno, pp. 560-561.

60. Zunes and Mundy, p. 9.

61. Fuente Cobo and Meriño Menéndez, p. 77.

62. *Ibid.*, 77-78.

63. *Ibid.*

64. *Ibid.*, p. 78. The account of a Moroccan doctor who was held prisoner by the Polisario for many years describes how, in at least one battle, Polisario soldiers customarily shot anyone whom they did not deem "useful." Thomas Hollowell, *Allah's Garden. A True Story of a Forgotten War in the Sahara Desert of Morocco*, Urbana, IL: Tales Press, 2009, pp. 45-48.

65. Fuente Cobo and Meriño Menéndez, p. 78.

66. Hacene-Djaballah, p. 43.

67. Fuente Cobo and Meriño Menéndez, p. 78.

68. *Ibid.*, pp. 78-79.

69. *Ibid,* p. 79.

70. *Ibid.*, 79-80; Zunes and Mundy, p. 11; Diego Aguirre, pp. 160-161.

71. Fuente Cobo and Meriño Menéndez, pp. 80-81.

72. *Ibid.*, pp. 80, 82.

73. Zunes and Mundy, p. 11; Diego Aguirre, p. 150; Fuente Cobo and Meriño Menéndez, p. 82.

74. Hacene-Djaballah, pp. 144-145.

75. *Ibid.*

76. Fuente Cobo and Meriño Menéndez, p. 87.

77. *Ibid.*, pp. 86-87; Mundy, "The Morocco-Polisario War," p. 223.

78. Diego Aguirre, pp. 221-222; Fuente Cobo and Meriño Menéndez, p. 89.

79. Fuente Cobo and Meriño Menéndez, p. 90.

80. Diego Aguirre, pp. 221-222.

81. Fuente Cobo and Meriño Menéndez, p. 93.

82. Mundy, "The Morocco-Polisario War," p. 219.

83. Diego Aguirre, p. 223.

84. *Ibid.*, pp. 223-224.

85. Mundy, "The Morocco-Polisario War," p. 219; Diego Aguirre, pp. 224-225.

86. Fuente Cobo and Meriño Menéndez, pp. 95-97.

87. *Ibid.*, p. 100.

88. Mundy, "The Morocco-Polisario War," p. 223.

89. Zunes and Mundy, p. 66.

90. *Ibid.*, pp. 17-20.

91. Mundy, "The Morocco-Polisario War," pp. 219-220.

92. Sobero, p. 58.

93. For example, see Fuente Cobo and Meriño Menéndez, p. 104.

94. Zunes and Mundy, p. 21.

95. *Ibid.*

96. Sobero, p. 59.

97. Zunes and Mundy, p. 21. Another account writes that construction of the first wall, extending from Draa to the Saac area, began in August 1980. Diego Aguirre, p. 230.

98. Fuente Cobo and Meriño Menéndez, pp. 104-108.

99. Mundy, "The Morocco-Polisario war," p. 222; Fuente Cobo and Meriño Menéndez, p. 108.

100. Zunes and Mundy, pp. 21-22; Fuente Cobo and Meriño Menéndez, p. 108; Sobero, pp. 58-59.

101. Fuente Cobo and Meriño Menéndez, p. 110.

102. *Ibid.*, pp. 110-112.

103. *Ibid.*, pp. 112-114.

104. *Ibid.*, p. 115.

105. Zunes and Mundy, pp. 22-23.

106. Fuente Cobo and Meriño Menéndez, p. 117.

107. Zunes and Mundy, p. 23.

108. *Ibid.*, p. 24.

109. Sobero, pp. 116-121; Zunes and Mundy, p. 149; Soto-Trillo, p. 73. See also Erik Jensen, *Western Sahara: Anatomy of a Stalemate*, 2nd Ed., Boulder, CO: Lynn Rienner, 2012. Jensen headed MINURSO from 1994 to 1998.

110. Anna Theofilopoulou, "Morocco's New Constitution and the Western Sahara Conflict—A Missed Opportunity?" *Journal of North African Studies*, 2012, pp. 1-10 (First Article), p. 5.

111. Alexis Arieff, "Western Sahara," *CRS Report for Congress*, April 5, 2012.

112. *Ibid.*; Zunes and Mundy, pp. 159, 229-239; Jensen, *Western Sahara*, pp. 6-7, 103.

113. "2012 Regional Operations Profile—North Africa," UNHCR, available from *www.unhcr.org/cgi-bin/texis/vtxpage?page =49e4861f6&submit=GO#*; Sobero, pp. 67-69.

114. "Los cooperantes afirman que la situación de los re-fugiados saharauis es 'crítica'" ("Aid workers assert that the situation of the Saharan refugees is 'critical'"), *El País*, August 13, 2012, available from *ccaa.elpais.com/ccaa/2012/08/13/andalucia/1344874803_831290.html*.

115. Alejandro García, *Historia del Sáhara. El Mejor y el Peor de los Mundos* (*The History of the Sahara: The Best and Worst of Worlds*), Madrid, Spain: Libros de la Catarata, 2001, pp. 331-332, cited in San Martín, *Western Sahara*, p. 111.

116. *Ibid.*; San Martín, *Western Sahara*, pp. 146-147.

117. Sobero, pp. 64-66; San Martín, *Western Sahara*, especially Chaps 3 and 4.

118. Soto-Trillo, p. 31.

119. San Martín, *Western Sahara*, p. 121.

120. Cited in Arieff, p. 4, Endnote 10. Also Soto-Trillo, pp. 189-191.

121. "Los cooperantes," *El País*.

122. San Martín, *Western Sahara*, pp. 130-132.

86

123. Soto-Trillo, pp. 134, 140, 176; San Martín, "´¡*Estos locos cubarauis!*'", pp. 249-263.

124. Soto-Trillo records many charges to this effect in his travel narrative, which is overall very sympathetic to the Sahrawi nationalist cause. For example, see pp. 181, 198, 212-221, 224, 233.

125. Boukhars and Amar, p. 222; Sobero, pp. 108-113; Soto-Trillo, pp. 196-207; Zunes and Mundy, p. 157.

126. Sobero, pp. 181-182.

127. *Ibid.*, pp. 175-180; Zunes and Mundy, pp. 145-147.

128. Sobero, p. 174.

129. *Ibid.*, pp. 184-189; Zunes and Mundy, p. 205.

130. Sobero, pp. 168-170.

131. Quoted in Arieff, pp. 4-5.

132. Moshe Gershovich, "Democratization in Morocco: Political Transition of a North African Kingdom," *Policy Brief*, No. 7, The Middle East Institute, February 2008, p. 7, available from *www.humansecuritygateway.com/documents/MEI_Morocco_democratizationpoliticaltransition.pdf*; Aida Alami, "Web Offers a Voice to Journalists in Morocco," *The New York Times*, April 28, 2011, available from *www.nytimes.com/2011/04/28/world/middleeast/28iht-M28C-MOROCCO-MEDIA.html*.

133. Theofilopoulou, pp. 1-10.

134. Sobero, pp. 193-198.

135. Zunes and Mundy, pp. 157-158.

136. *Ibid.*, p. 140.

137. For two distinct accounts of the causes, course, and outcome of the November 2010 events, see Boukhars and Amar; and,

Jacob Mundy, "Western Sahara's 48 Hours of Rage," *Middle East Report*, No. 257, Winter 2010, available from *www.merip.org/mer/ mer257/western-saharas-48-hours-rage*.

138. Mundy, "Western Sahara's 48 Hours."

139. Boukhars and Amar, p. 231.

140. Zunes and Mundy, p. 158.

141. Sobero, pp. 168-175; Zunes and Mundy, pp. 144, 151-154.

142. Zunes and Mundy, pp. 151-152.

143. *Ibid.*, p. 155.

144. *Ibid.*, pp. 140-141, 152-153.

145. Soto-Trillo, pp. 169, 237-238; Zunes and Mundy, p. 159.

146. Sobero, p. 172; Soto-Trillo, pp. 246, 268.

147. "Arab Spring Started in Western Sahara," *Deutsche Welle*, June 18, 2012, available from *www.dw.de/dw/article/0,, 16033135,00.html*.

148. Quoted in J. Peter Pham, "Foreign Influences and Shifting Horizons: The Ongoing Evolution of al Queda in the Islamic Maghreb," *Orbis*, Spring 2011, p. 249.

149. Arieff, p. 5.

150. Boukhars and Amar, pp. 224-226.

151. Soto-Trillo, p. 142.

152. Fernando Reinares, "Condominio 'yihadista' en el norte de Mali" ("Jihadist Condominium in the North of Mali"), *El Pais*, August 11, 2012, available from *elpais.com/elpais/2012/07/26 /opinion/1343296013_792031.html*.

153. Pham, pp. 240-254.

154. Carlos Ruiz Miguel, "Sáhara Occidental 1975-2005: Cambio de Variables de un Conflicto Estancado" ("Western Sahara 1975-2005: Change of Variables in a Conflict at a Standstill"), *ARI* N. 40, March 30, 2005 (Report of the Real Instituto Elcano de Estudios Internacionales y Estratégicos), available from *www. realinstitutoelcano.org/wps/portal/rielcano/contenido?WCM_ GLOBAL_CONTEXT=/elcano/elcano_es/zonas_es/mediterraneo+y+- mundo+arabe/ari+40-2005.*

155. "Los cooperantes," *El País*.

156. Arieff, p. 5.

157. Renata Capella Soler, "Los derechos humanos, ¿un obstáculo para la paz en el Sáhara Occidental?" ("Human rights: an obstacle to peace in the Western Sahara?"), *ARI* N. 47, March 8, 2011 (Report of Real Instituto Elcano de Estudios Internacionales y Estratégicos), available from *www.realinstitutoelcano.org/wps/ portal/rielcano/contenido?WCM_GLOBAL_CONTEXT=/elcano/ elcano_es/zonas_es/organismos+internacionales/ari47-2011.*

158. Anna Khakee, "The Western Saharan Autonomy Proposal and Political Reform in Morocco," *NOREF Report*, June 2011, available from *www.peacebuilding.no/var/ezflow_site/storage/ original/application/a3acc871f1198e8e21bfc68ae75f8f48.pdf.*

159. See *www.africom.mil/oef-ts.asp.*

160. Roberto Benito, "España estudia participar con tropas en una misión internacional en Mali" ("Spain Considers Participating with Troops in an International Mission in Mali"), *El Mundo*, July 30, 2012, p. 5.

161. Theofilopoulou, p. 2.

162. Benito.

U.S. ARMY WAR COLLEGE

Major General Anthony A. Cucolo III
Commandant

*****

STRATEGIC STUDIES INSTITUTE
and
U.S. ARMY WAR COLLEGE PRESS

Director
Professor Douglas C. Lovelace, Jr.

Director of Research
Dr. Steven K. Metz

Author
Dr. Geoffrey Jensen

Editor for Production
Dr. James G. Pierce

Publications Assistant
Ms. Rita A. Rummel

*****

Composition
Mrs. Jennifer E. Nevil